THE BASICS OF

PROCESS MAPPING

2nd Edition

THE BASICS OF

PROCESS MAPPING

2nd Edition

Robert Damelio

CRC Press
Taylor & Francis Group
Boca Raton   London   New York

CRC Press is an imprint of the
Taylor & Francis Group, an **informa** business

A PRODUCTIVITY PRESS BOOK

Productivity Press
711 Third Avenue
New York, NY 10017

© 2011 by Robert Damelio
Productivity Press is an imprint of Taylor & Francis Group, an Informa business

No claim to original U.S. Government works

Printed in the United States of America on acid-free paper

International Standard Book Number: 978-1-56327-376-6 (Paperback)

Library of Congress Cataloging-in-Publication Data

Damelio, Robert.
    The basics of process mapping / Robert Damelio. -- 2nd ed.
       p. cm.
    ISBN 978-1-56327-376-6 (acid-free paper)
    1. Work design. 2. Flow charts. 3. Organizational effectiveness. I. Title.

T60.8.D36 2011
658.5'4--dc22   2010006278

Visit the Taylor & Francis Web site at
http://www.taylorandfrancis.com

and the CRC Press Web site at
http://www.crcpress.com

Contents

Chapter 1

Overview

In this chapter, I'll explain why I wrote the first edition of this book and introduce each of the three types of maps that I've included in the book.

Why I Wrote the Basics of Process Mapping

At the time, (1996) I'd already been working well over a decade to help improve the results that organizations achieve from the work that their people do. As part of that work, I'd personally created custom learning materials on a variety of quality improvement tools, methods, and procedures. Many of these included "how-to" guidance and job aids.

Also during that time, I found the Three Levels of Performance framework that I learned from Geary Rummler to be particularly useful and effective. I still do.

The Three Levels Framework helps one "view" work at the organization, process, and job/performer levels (Table 1.1). At the organization and process levels, Rummler introduced two key maps (**relationship maps** and **cross-functional process maps**, respectively) to help diagnose and improve work.

Table 1.1 Level of Performance and Map Type

Level of Performance	Map Used	"View" of Work Emphasized
Organization	Relationship map	**Organization:** The supplier–customer relationships that exist between "parts" of an organization
Process	Cross-functional process map, also known as a "swimlane diagram"	**Workflow:** The *path* of work that "crosses" several functions, plus the *architecture* that connects the relevant activities, people, information systems, and other resources along that path
Job/Performer	Flowchart	**Activity:** The value-creating or nonvalue-creating work performed

Many of my clients asked for "something on process maps," and so this book was born. *The Basics of Process Mapping* contains how-to guidance and examples for three types of maps, one for each of the Three Levels of Performance* (see footnote on flowcharts below).

When I wrote the first edition, I noticed that many of the quality or process improvement tools and examples were most often illustrated in manufacturing settings, but the growth in jobs (work) was occurring *outside of* manufacturing settings.

For this reason, I used *nonmanufacturing* work examples and language throughout the book to illustrate how these three maps apply. Over the years, this trend has accelerated such that service and knowledge work are now the predominant forms of work in the economies of the "developed" nations worldwide.

Timing is everything.

---

* Rummler did not include flowcharts as one of the three levels maps. I have included flowcharts and related them to the Job/Performer level of performance.

Key Features of Each Map:
A Preview of What's Coming

Beginning on the following page, I've included an overview of the key features for these three map types:

- Relationship map
- Cross-functional process map also known as swimlane diagram
- Flowchart

What Constitutes a "Key" Feature?

A key feature distinguishes one map type from another *and* would generally be thought of as a "recognized signature" or trademark in a map of that type.

What Is a Relationship Map?

A **relationship map** visually depicts the "**parts**" of an **Organization**, and the *internal* or *external* **supplier-customer relationships** among those parts. It follows a general left to right (resource conversion) sequence represented by the same three components: Suppliers, the Organization, and Customers. It does not explicitly show work activities. Rather, it shows the input/output connections or linkages among *selected parts* of the organization. (The rectangle symbol represents a cluster of resources and activities that often represent departments or functions, i.e. structural building blocks of that organization).

This map is sometimes referred to as an "organization relationship map."

Key Features of Relationship Maps

Here are three key features of relationship maps (see Figure 1.1)

 A. Supplier-Organization-Customer (throughput sequence)
  - An organization is one link in a broader value-chain; it exists within a broader system
  - Organizations "take in" resources (from suppliers). They convert or transform those resources into another *customer valued* form (output).
 B. Part/Whole relationships
  - In systems thinking terms, the "parts" are components; they are also subsets of a *whole* (set) of like components.
  - Another way to think of a "part" is as a *portion* of the *whole* (entire) work that the organization performs
 C. Supplier-customer relationships
  - Organizations (work systems) are made up of *interdependent* components
  - A supplier-customer relationship is a type of interdependency between one organization part (component) and another

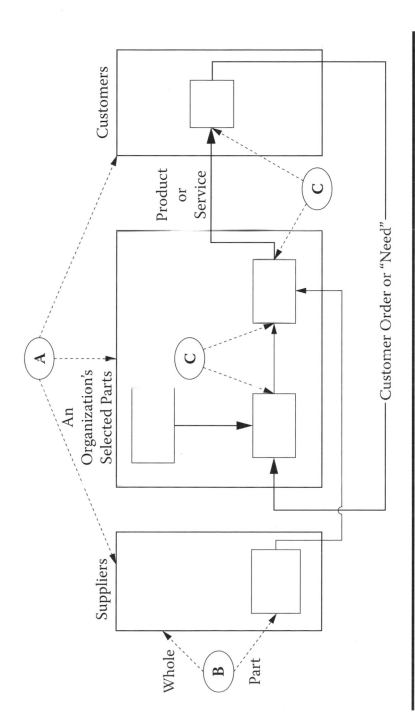

Figure 1.1 Relationship map—Key features: (A) Supplier–organization–customer "throughput" pattern, (B) part/whole relationship, (C) supplier–customer relationships.

What Is a Cross-Functional Process Map or Swimlane Diagram?

A **cross-functional process** map illustrates **workflow** in organizations. A work-flow consists of a set and series of interrelated work activities and resources that follow a distinct path as work inputs (resources) get transformed into outputs (items) that customer's value. The name, "**cross-functional process map**" means the *whole* (end-to-end) work process "crosses" several functions or other organization entities.

It also called a **swimlane diagram** because the pattern of the horizontal bands is similar to the lanes of an Olympic swimming pool (as seen from *above* the pool).

Whereas the relationship map only shows the **parts** of an organization, the cross-functional process map shows you the work that takes place within in each part. Note that the rectangles that represent **organization "parts"** on a relationship map **become horizontal bands or "swimlanes"** on the cross-functional process map.

Key Features of Cross-Functional Process Maps

Here are three key features of cross-functional process maps (see Figure 1.2)

A. Swimlane
  • The horizontal band shows work activities in the *context* of the organization part or other "entity" that holds or performs those activities
B. Workflow
  • A set of interrelated activities and resources deployed in a unique manner
  • This is the mechanism that creates and delivers value
C. Supplier-customer relationships
  • Handoff of work *item* between two distinct entities
  • In systems thinking terms, this (handoff) is an *interface between two components*

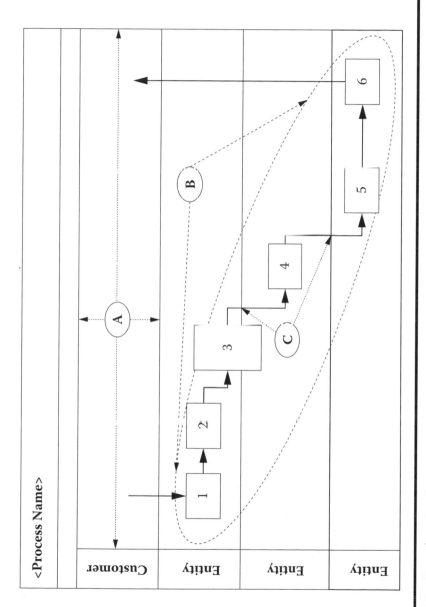

Figure 1.2 Cross-functional process map—Key Featurres: (A) "Swimlane" (entity), (B) workflow, (C) "handoff" (*internal supplier–customer relationship*).

What Is a Flowchart?

A flowchart is a graphic representation of the sequence of work **activities** used to create, produce, or provide a *single* specific, unique output. It may be used to categorize work activities as value creating or non value creating. Of the three maps in this book, I use the flowchart to represent the most granular view of work.

Key Features of Flowcharts

Here are two key features of flowcharts (see Figure 1.3)

A. Value creating activity
- <u>One</u> symbol is used to represent work that transforms a resource into a form that *customer's* value and for which they would willingly pay

B. Non value-creating activity
- *A set of different symbols* are used to make the *types of waste* in the non value-creating activity *visible*, such as delays, storage, batching, movement, inspection, approval, rework, etc.
- Work that *consumes* resources and time, but does not *transform* the resource (would be "seen" as *waste* by the customer)

Now that I've introduced the key features of these three maps, let's take a closer look at how we may use them to learn more about the work each map represents.

Three Views of the Same Work

To help you better understand how the three types of maps in this book may be used an integrated set, I've created three "views" of the **same work** using a relationship map, a swimlane diagram (cross-functional process map), and a flowchart.

Introduction to Phil's Quick Lube

I'll be using a service business example of Phil's Quick Lube to illustrate each of the three maps that this book contains.

Phil's Quick Lube (Phil's) provides preventive maintenance services for your vehicle. Preventive maintenance (PM) includes services tailored to specific systems and components of your vehicle such as electrical, engine, transmission, cooling, etc. Typical PM services include:

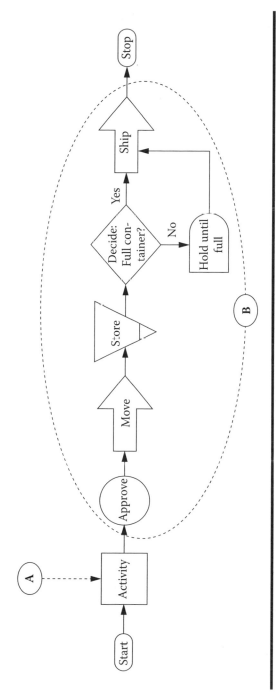

Figure 1.3 Flowchart—Key features: (A) Value-creating activity, (B) nonvalue-creating activities.

1. Checking, maintaining, or replacing the battery
2. Performing oil changes
3. Replacing transmission fluid and filter
4. Checking cooling systems and replenishing fluids

In addition to the preventive maintenance lines of business, Phil's is a licensed provider of annual Texas State Motor Vehicle inspections. Phil's does not do repairs per se.

Phil's provides these services quickly (fast turnaround) and usually with little or no waiting. Two of the higher volume services are oil changes and vehicle inspections.

Overview of an Oil Change: Work Sequence

Here is the main sequence of work activities associated with an oil change:

1. Greet customer
2. Write service order
3. Position vehicle in appropriate service bay
4. Prepare vehicle and supplies
5. Perform the oil change
6. Affix reminder sticker on windshield
7. Perform quality check
8. Position vehicle in pick-up area
9. Prepare and present invoice
10. Collect payment

What would the oil change work look like using each of the three maps (see Figure 1.4)?

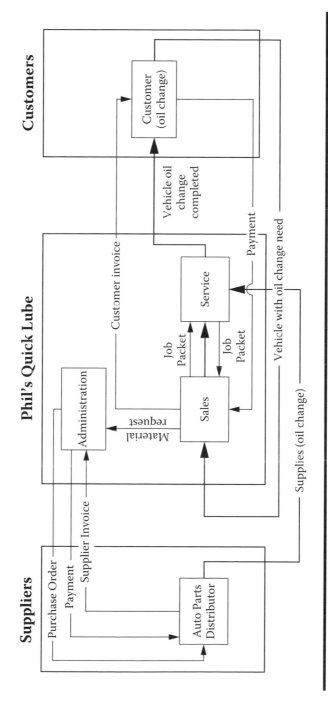

Figure 1.4 Organization view of Phil's Quick Lube oil change using relationship map.

Organization View of Oil Change

First, look at the relationship **map** (Figure 1.4) **as a whole** and note that it shows a *set* of *external* Suppliers on the left, a *set* of *external* Customers on the right, and a *set* of Organization parts (called Phil's Quick Lube) in the middle. This Supplier, Organization, Customer pattern is the same for all (Enterprise level) relationship maps. Think of this pattern as the default template to use when you draw a relationship map.

Next, note the **part(s)** present. (look inside the default template) There are five in all. Within the *set* of Suppliers, we see one type of Supplier-an auto parts distributor. Within the *set* of Organization parts known as Phil's Quick Lube, we see three parts: Administration, Sales, and Service. Within the *set* of Customers, we see one type-an oil change Customer.

How does each part "fit in" with the other parts? What contribution does each part make to an Oil Change?

To answer these questions we focus on *linkages*. By linkages I mean the flow of inputs and outputs and how they *connect one part to another* shown in the map.

Let's trace the *transformation of the main resource input* (the vehicle that needs an oil change). You can see that the Customer, Sales, and Service parts are involved, i.e. a vehicle with a need for an oil change is an output of the Customer and an input into Sales. Coming out of Sales, the vehicle is now an input into Service. Then, when the vehicle leaves Service, we see that the oil change has been completed.

You can see the *logical* (but not actual) path of the vehicle, the parts involved along the path, the result of each part's involvement, and the *state change* of the vehicle as it progresses along the path.

There are two other linkages (supplier-customer relationships) between Sales and the Customer. We see an invoice going to the Customer and a payment coming from the Customer to Sales.

In addition to the vehicle, there are two more linkages between Sales and Service. Something called a job packet goes from Sales to Service, and then, from Service to Sales.

Now let's take a look at the linkages between the auto parts distributor and the different parts of Phil's Quick Lube. We see the auto parts distributor providing supplies to Service, probably in response to the Purchase Order they received from Administration. Then it seems the auto parts distributor sends an invoice to Administration, and then Administration sends a payment to the auto parts distributor.

So, where are the 10 work activities associated with an oil change?

They don't show up explicitly because they are work *activities*.

Generally, a <u>relationship map shows parts, but does not show the work activity that occurs within each part</u> of the organization. In this (organization) view of work the (oil change) activities are embedded within the Sales and Service "parts" of the organization.

How would the same work appear in a *cross-functional process* map or *swim-lane diagram*?

Workflow View of Oil Change

Whenever you see or show a cross-functional process map (Figure 1.5) to someone else *in conjunction with a relationship map*, keep in mind or point out that in the workflow view of work, the **rectangles are work activities**.

In a relationship map, the rectangles were "parts." In a cross-functional process map, the "parts" are still there and visible, but now they *appear as horizontal bands or swimlanes*. This view shows work activities *within the context* of a particular workflow, and within the organization part (or other entity) responsible for doing that work.

So the 10 activities we started with are readily apparent; from the *swimlanes* we also see which parts (from the relationship map) are responsible for each activity. Three more activities are now visible as well. These activities involve purchasing, providing, and paying for supplies.

The mystery of the job packet is solved. We now know that it contains the service order and car keys, and is part of the handoff between Sales and Service. The job packet stays with the vehicle until the oil change sequence (3 to 8) is completed. Then the job packet is returned to Sales where it is used to create the invoice.

What would this work look like using a flowchart?

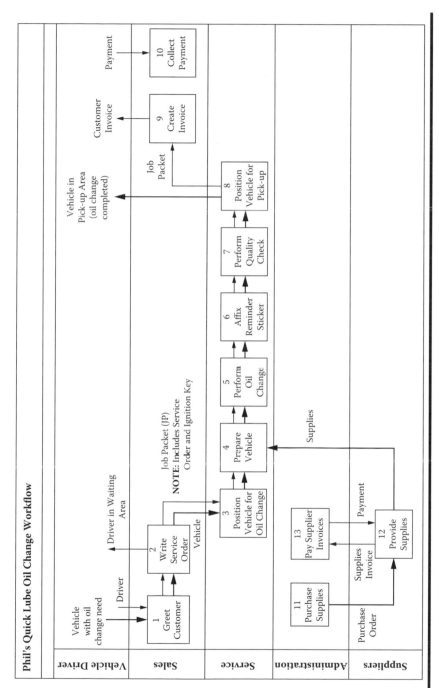

Figure 1.5   Workflow view of Phil's Quick Lube oil change using a cross-functional process map.

Activity View of Oil Change

Believe it or not, this (Figure 1.6, Figure 1.7, and Figure 1.8) is the work associated with one activity, "Write Service Order (Activity 2)," from the workflow view (Figure 1.5). This is the most granular level of detail, i.e. the "ground truth" view of work (which is why I am limiting the work shown via flowchart to a single activity).

What the activity view shows is that the work of Activity 2 is a long sequence made of a few value creating steps, along with a combination of decisions, delays, and lots of walking.

In other words, a typical day at the office!

I'll elaborate on each map in Chapters 4, 5, and 6, respectively.

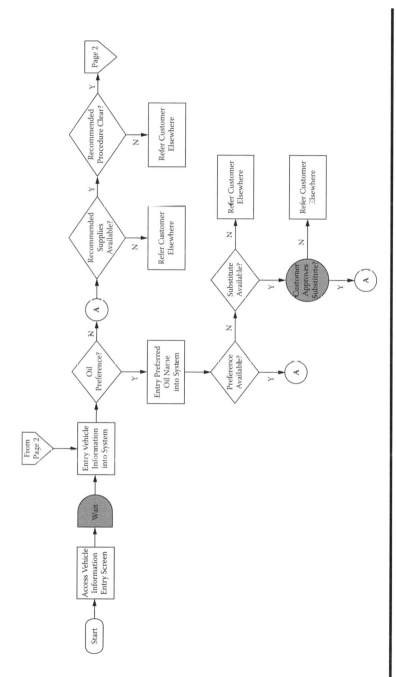

Figure 1.6 Activity view of Phil's Quick Lube oil change (Activity 2: Write service order) using a flowchart.

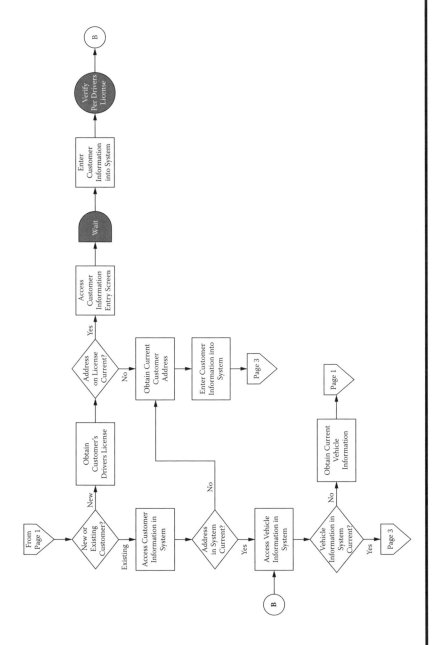

Figure 1.7 Activity view of Phil's Quick Lube oil change (Activity 2: Write service order) using a flowchart.

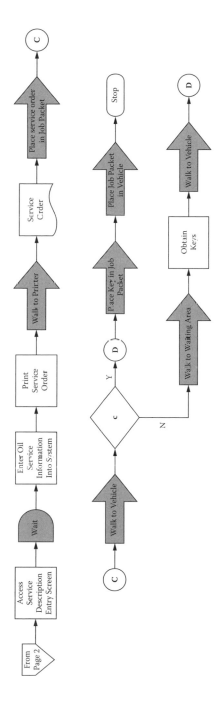

Figure 1.8 Activity view of Phil's Quick Lube oil change (Activity 2: Write service order) using a flowchart.

Chapter 2

Thinking about Work

Overview

In this chapter, I'm providing "working definitions" of several key concepts I use when thinking about, or describing, "work" so you'll understand what I had in mind as I wrote this material. I especially use the words "workflow" and "flow" in ways that may not be consistent with how you've seen these words used elsewhere.

Since this book is on the basics of process mapping, I'm limiting what I say about these concepts to the working definitions plus a brief statement explaining why I think the concepts matter. At the conclusion of the chapter, I've included a list of assumptions based on this terminology as well.

Here is how I've organized this chapter:

- What is "work?"
- What is a work "component?"
- What is a work "boundary?"
- What is a work "feature?"
- What is a "property" of work?
- (Process) Maps as models of work
- What is a process?
- What is a workflow?
- What is *flow*?
- What is a value stream?
- List of selected assumptions regarding work

What Is Work?

When you think of *work*, what comes to mind?

One of the lessons I've learned is that, though most of us have experience with *work* (we currently work, know someone who works, or once did), the ways in which we think and talk about *work* often differ dramatically.

Let's start with the following:

> **Work** is the "exertion of effort to directed to produce or accomplish something."*

You could even reduce this further perhaps to "purposeful activity."

Why (How We Define Work) Matters

Our *mental model* of "work" (the image that comes to mind when we *think* about work, and the language we use to describe or communicate that image of work) shapes our ability to make meaningful improvements to that work. By meaningful, I mean changes to work that customers' value.

For example, if you think of work primarily in terms of "purposeful activity," chances are good that to improve work, you'll focus on activities in some way, and perhaps consider that the purpose of those activities is to create value for customers.

If we are trying to perform, improve, measure, or manage "work," we should first reach agreement on what constitutes "work."

More importantly, <u>what is it about that work that we should attend to</u> (and why) when trying to perform, improve, measure, or manage that work?

I believe a useful way to answer this question *always* involves making changes or adjustments to some combination of the components, boundaries, features, and properties of the work.

What Is a Work Component?

A work component is an activity or resource that serves as a constituent part or element of work. They are the "building blocks" of work.

Components do not "stand alone," (they just appear to do so).

---

* work. (n.d.). *Dictionary.com Unabridged*. From Dictionary.com Web site: http://dictionary. reference.com/browse/work (accessed December 30, 2009).

To be considered as a component, an activity or resource must be an interdependent part of a larger and uniquely identifiable, whole. It takes a set of components to create something that no component individually may produce (the result of the whole differs from those of its parts).

In other words, it is the <u>relationship that exists</u> between activities or resources and the purpose or intended result from their use, which determines whether or not they may be considered to be components. For example, I would consider each *activity* within a sequential series of interrelated activities in a process to be components *of that particular* process. One type of relationship is interdependency; another is part/whole.

Examples of Work Components

Activities	Tasks, steps, acts, actions, deeds, accomplishments, or achievements that expend effort and occur in the workplace	
Resources	Input (to an activity) that is converted or transformed into a customer-valued item (via the activity or a series of activities). The <u>form</u> of the resource <u>changes</u>.	The specific form of the resource being acted upon to create the valued work item. Iron ore is an input to steel. A vehicle needing an oil change is an input to the process that "changes" the oil.
	Applied during or used to perform activities. The form of the resource does *not* change.	Tools, labor, IT, information, methods, knowledge, energy, etc.
	Applied or used to support or enable an activity to occur; provides conditions so that activity may take place. The form does *not* change.	Facility, training, HVAC, lighting, etc.
Structural	Alternatives used to organize a group of activities and resources	Job, department, function, team, project, program, or other organizational "unit"

Why Work Components Matter

Interactions among the components determine the performance of a system (or of a process, workflow, or value stream).

By thinking of *work* this way, it both prompts and allows us to examine the connections between and among the set of interdependent components used to do the work.

It also helps us identify or define the most relevant context within which any given component may best be evaluated.

When you next encounter an activity or resource, here are some questions to consider: What is the relevant context within which I should view this activity? What is the relevant set of components within that context? How effective are the linkages among that set? How do the components interact with one another? What affect does this interaction have on (job, process, or function) performance? Have the components been explicitly designed to operate as an integrated whole?

What Is a Work Boundary?

A work boundary is a border or limit to the size or scope of work activities or resources.

Boundaries define where work starts or stops and how much (what amount of work) is in-between.

Every component of work has boundaries.

Work boundaries are often both intangible and arbitrary, but they nonetheless exist.

Boundaries act as interfaces between components. Resources and information often must pass through these interfaces. A classic example would be a "handoff" of work between two distinct jobs, each of which is in a different department.

Example of Selected Work Boundaries

The beginning and ending of a process, of each activity within that process; of each resource component used, transformed, or applied within that process are all boundaries. Jobs have boundaries, so do databases.

Why Work Boundaries Matter

If work were a jigsaw puzzle, then the puzzle pieces would be work components. Each piece has boundaries. Suppose this same puzzle is available in either of two configurations: 5 pieces, and 15 pieces. Which is less complex? Which takes longer to complete? Which has more possibilities to make mistakes? Now suppose the work of a given work process may be done by 5 people or 15 people. Ask the same "puzzle" questions.

More boundaries mean more interfaces and greater complexity. Complexity adds more cost, creates more opportunities for errors, requires more coordination to align and synchronize the components, and increases the lead-time to complete the work.

What Is a Work Feature?

A feature of work is "a prominent or conspicuous part or characteristic." Features of work are generally visible and observable.

Work components have features, individually and collectively.

Example of Work Features

Supplier-Customer relationships, handoffs, the type and effectiveness of connections between or among components, (such as whether components are synchronized or aligned with one another) part/whole relationships, the location or proximity of required resources, workflow (architecture) design, workflow activity patterns (serial, collaborative, or parallel), and activity dependency relationships are all features of work.

Why Features Matter

Components have features individually and collectively. We are most interested in how features either help or hinder item flow, and create value or waste.

I describe problematic components and features that frequently occur in knowledge work and business processes in Chapter 7.

What Is Work Property?

A work property is "a characteristic attribute possessed by all members of a class."

Example of Selected Work Properties

Customer-perceived value, quality, flow, size, variation, and cost are widely used properties of work. Organizations differ in the weight or priority they assign to each property.

Why Work Properties Matter

These are measurable attributes of work. When you "change" or "improve" work, it will affect one or more of these properties. We can quantify the results of changes and improvements to work using these properties.

Now that I've defined and shown you examples of work properties I have a way to distinguish between two categories of work activities, based on the work property of customer-perceived value.

All activities use resources and are considered "work."

Those activities that consume resources and turn those resources into forms that customers value, are called value-creating activities.

Those activities that use resources for some other purpose, we call non value-creating activities, or more commonly, *waste*.

(Process) Maps Are Models of Work

I think of the three maps in the book as models that provide a different view of work. Each map (model) depicts the boundaries, selected components, features, and properties of work in some way (using specific symbols and conventions). In Chapters 4, 5, and 6 I identify and describe many of these symbols and conventions that each map type typically uses.

What Is (Work Viewed as) a Process?

For a working definition of "process," I use the definition below, courtesy of Alec Sharp, a colleague who is both an experienced practitioner and accomplished author. By the way, I highly recommend his book, Workflow Modeling, to those who want more in-depth information on swimlane diagrams.

"a business process is a collection of interrelated activities, initiated in response to triggering event, which achieves a specific, discrete result for the customer and other stakeholders of the process '"

When you look at (observe) work, what do you see?

I used to see people, artifacts, and activity. How about you?

Where is the *process*? I contend that you really don't see a process you see *work*.

More specifically, you see primarily what I refer to as components and features of work. The people, artifacts, and activity are still there, but the *workflow context* for those components is generally not visible (unless your organization is well along in its "Lean transformation.") The ways in which the *relevant* components are deployed, how they operate, and how they connect to one another exhibit features that help or hinder "flow," and create value or waste.

Stated slightly differently, if something is a component, its relevance, function, or contribution occurs *only within the context of the system* or *workflow* (as I use the term) to which it "belongs."

What Is (Work Viewed as) a Workflow?

To think about work as a "workflow," I'll start with the above definition of "process."

The boundaries of our workflow begin with the activity that immediately follows the "triggering event;" they end with the activity whose output is the "specific, discrete result." I use the word "*item*" as synonym for the "specific, discrete result." Each one of our "collection of interrelated activities," involves several resources, occurs in a specific sequence and has some form of linkage to the next activity, and to other resources.

I use the term "workflow" to refer to the *architecture* of everything I just described in the preceding paragraph, and especially to the *actual* path the work *item* follows as it evolves from the initial resource input, gets transformed by each of the activities, and becomes the work *item* that exits the workflow.

Each work item has is its own workflow.

---

* Alec Sharp, *Workflow Modeling, 2nd edition*, Artech House 2009, 56.

What Is "Flow?"

"Flow" is the work *property* that characterizes the evolution or transformation of the resource input into the work item along the actual path within the workflow.

It's tempting to think of "flow" as the progression or movement of work along the path. This generally is considered waste, since *movement* of work does not create more value in that work.

The ideal *state* of "flow" is *continuous* and consists of 100 percent value-creating activities. Each item gets created from start to finish with no delays, defects, waster, or work in process inventory. In "Lean speak" this is called, "one-piece, continuous flow."

What Is (Work Viewed as) a Value Stream?

To go from workflow (as I use the term) to value stream we use the architecture as a blueprint for actual operation. We make the item and it's "path" explicitly visible, and *deploy, operate, and connect all remaining components so that they work collectively to optimize the flow of the item* (through the value stream). We build in real-time measurement and feedback related to item flow and to actual customer demand. We operate and manage the value stream as an *integrated whole*, that is, as a *distinct* value-creating and delivery *system* whose *purpose* is "one piece, continuous flow" of a defect free item, created right before it goes to the customer at the time they expect.

I have created material on value stream maps that is similar in design to the "map" chapters in this book (Chapters 4, 5, or 6), that you may view at http://basicsofprocessmapping.com/

Some Assumptions Regarding Work

1. Work consists of multiple components; they may be categorized into activities, resources, and structural. Of greater interest is the specific form each component takes, what features does it exhibit, and to which workflow it is most relevant.
2. There is no minimum "correct" number, type, mix, or amount of work components. Organizations often define or approach the same work in very different ways.
3. Work components are usually created as stand alone entities, often by separate departments that do not have a "shared mental model" of how the value-creating work of the organization takes place. Over time,

components tend to become personalized by the people who do the work. Both of these situations cause various forms of workflow "fragmentation" and act as barriers to flow.

4. There is no naturally occurring force in organizations to prevent workflow fragmentation, nor is there a natural force of cohesion to attract or keep related components together. Addressing this issue is one important reason for having process owners, or value steam managers or some role with the responsibility for establishing and maintaining the architecture of the workflow.

5. Often work components are not connected, or not effectively connected to other components that they affect, or by which they are affected. Weak or missing linkages among components affect how those components interact. The interactions among those components may or may not be a positive contributor to the system's performance. Often components will hinder one another; they may even have unintended consequences that show up in unexpected and inconvenient ways. Their collective impact is much less than it could or should be.

6. Different work components may be used at different points in time; some may be used once, some infrequently, some periodically, others everyday or even more often.

7. Each component has an effect on (contributes to, or causes) workflow or process performance; the effects are not equal. The relative impact of each component is determined to a large degree by how a given individual uses, interacts with, or is influenced by that component. These interactions and components are the sources and causes of variation in a process. They also help or hinder flow, and affect resource utilization.

8. There is a mismatch between current approaches for the design of work and the prevalent or default ways to structure organizations where the work occurs. One of the biggest mismatches occurs between job design and workflow design. Jobs (and most other structural components) typically are not designed with their contribution to workflows in mind. This violates my HTF rule. (How things "fit," determines how things "flow.")

Chapter 3

Why Map a Process?

Overview

In the previous chapter, I mentioned that I think of the maps in this book as models of work. In this chapter, I discuss reasons to map a process and expand upon the maps as models theme.

Why Map a Process?

Maps and flowcharts help make **work** *visible*. Or, at the very least, they make some aspect of that work visible.

The short answer to why map a process goes something like this. You map a process to add to your knowledge about the work the map represents so that you may apply that knowledge in order to achieve a specific goal or other intended purpose. Ideally the goal or purpose is explicit, and its intent is to measurably improves the business. Finally, the goal is well understood, and agreed upon by the people who are doing the mapping.

Reasons to Map a Process (Part 1)

Here are the main reasons why I would (help someone) map a process.

1. Help those responsible for doing the work "converge" upon the use of language and strengthen their shared mental models regarding:
   a. How to think about the work they do.
   b. How to improve that work in light of what the customer values about that work.
2. Level-set each member of the natural workgroup regarding the *context* of the work they do. I think there are three contexts each member of the work group should understand and internalize:
   a. Contribution to external customer value.
   b. Part/whole workflow relationships.
   c. Contribution or relationship to the primary workflow of the enterprise, i.e., the Order to Delivery or Order to Cash throughput sequence.
3. Make the work *architecture* (its boundaries, components, features, and properties) visible as a catalyst for subsequent action to:
   a. Improve, measure, monitor, or perform the work.
   b. Define or pilot alternative architectures for the work (organizing around flow, in particular).
   c. Assign ongoing ownership of the workflow.
4. Improve communication and understanding throughout the natural workgroup by highlighting what to pay attention to and why, perhaps as part of team building or cross-training activities.
5. Codify knowledge related to the work. When used this way, a process map may be one of a *set of* documents that collectively describe the best-known way to do this work currently. The documents may be called process descriptions, process-related assets, knowledge assets, standard work, procedures, work instructions, etc. I would expect all the work-related documentation to be maintained and revised as part of "daily work" for the relevant process owner or value stream manager and reside in some form of repository or process asset library.
6. Establish or make changes to the Enterprise-level workflow (process) architecture.
   a. Provide context for ongoing process improvement and process management.
   b. Clarify the implications of a "local" change on the main workflows of the Enterprise.
   c. Visualize part/whole relationships (how does this work "fit in" with other work).

Reasons to Map a Process (Part 2)

Many of my clients sought my assistance as they undertook major process improvement or change initiatives, such as:

■ **Quality Management**
   – AS9100 Quality Management System (QMS)—an aerospace industry standard
   – Total Quality Management (TQM)

■ **IT Deployment or Implementation**
   – Enterprise Resource Planning (ERP), i.e., SAP or Oracle
   – Enterprise-wide project management, i.e., Primavera

■ **Software Development/Systems Engineering Process Improvement**
   – Capability Maturity Model (CMM)
   – Capability Maturity Model Integration (CMMI)

■ **Continuous Improvement**
   – Rummler–Brache three levels framework
   – Benchmarking
   – Business Process Improvement (BPI)
   – Six Sigma
   – Lean, TPS, Lean Six Sigma

■ **Measurement/Strategy**
   – Balanced Scorecard

How Do the Two Lists of Reasons Compare?

I don't think the reasons conflict with each other or that one list is somehow better than the other. I do think there may be differing motivations or philosophies between the two. For instance, a common theme with the first list is ongoing people development. The purpose may be to strengthen the understanding within each member of a natural work group regarding how their work contributes to customer value and to the business. With the second list, a common underlying theme is *process thinking*, or *process focus*. The general goal may be to improve process performance via the application of a systematic and standardized approach.

What's interesting is that each of the approaches in the second list has its own jargon and core beliefs regarding the best (preferred) way to improve a work process. Stated differently, though the work is the same, each approach targets a *different set* of work components, features, and properties; "frames" a problem with the current state of that set; and offers a solution to address the causes of the problem. To make matters worse, different language is often used to describe the same work phenomena. I know this from first-hand experience.

I believe that the range of approaches that many organizations are using creates a strong need for process improvement professionals to be "tool agnostic" and fluent in several improvement dialects. This would position these improvement practitioners to serve as trusted advisors or coaches to business leaders rather than true believers that specialize in the one best way they know to improve work.

Whether the reason for creating a process map comes from Part 1, Part 2, or elsewhere, when you create a process map, you are creating a **model** that is a **symbolic representation of work** *viewed as a process*.

What Is a Model?

Here is what I mean when I use the word *model*.*

> A schematic description of a system, theory, or phenomenon that accounts for its known or inferred properties and may be used for further study of its characteristics—*a model of generative grammar, a model of an atom, an economic model.*

Why Create a Model of Work?

A model of work should provide one or more of these benefits (adapted from *Visualizing Project Management)*[†]:

- Help to explain how work works.
- Broaden our perspective regarding work.
- Provide a common conceptual frame of reference about work.
- Express rules, guidelines, or principles related to work more simply.
- Clarify relationships, identify key elements, and consciously eliminate confusion factors concerning work.

---

* Model. (n.d.). *The American Heritage® dictionary of the English language, 4th ed.* Dictionary. com Web site: http://dictionary.reference.com/browse/model (accessed January 14, 2008).

[†] Kevin Forsberg et al. 2000. *Visualizing project management.* New York: John Wiley & Sons, p. 14.

(Process) Maps as *Models* of Work

We also should expect the work models we use to *account for the known or inferred properties* of work, and to help us better understand characteristics of work. Since I wrote the first edition of this book, I've come to understand that properties and characteristics (features) of work are a really big deal. When I started writing this edition, I realized that many of the maps (and symbols) we use to model work emphasize a *limited* set of boundaries, components, features, and properties of work, at best.

With the above in mind and in keeping with George Box's observation that, "essentially, all models are wrong, but some are useful,"* I contend that:

■ Maps show some things and not others.
■ No map shows all things (everything that may be of interest).
■ There is no such thing as the perfect map, or a map type that is inherently right, wrong, or best (except, of course, the ones that you or I draw).
■ You or your organization can *needlessly* spend a lot of time and money trying to "finish or complete" a map or set of maps.

It may seem strange that I mention the last point (because I've been paid to create maps), but I see no reason to keep working on a map when:

■ You have learned all that you need to about the work to make changes to it.
■ You are trying to guide "how-to" performance, in which case, procedures, job aids, training, another form of knowledge asset, or some combination may be more appropriate.

If a process map is a model of work, how does the work show up in the model?

When we create a process map, we use symbols and conventions to represent work boundaries and to highlight *selected* components, features, and properties of the work within those boundaries. The set of symbols used to represent an input, activity, and output sequence is known as the I-P-O (input, process, output) model, shown in Figure 3.1.

The arrows represent the input to, and output from a work activity, as well as the direction of the resource transformation or conversion sequence. The rectangle represents the actions taken during the activity to transform or act upon the resource input in some way.

---

* http://en.wikiquote.org/w/index.php?title=George_E._P._Box&oldid=754544

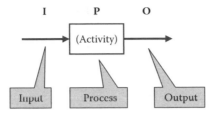

Figure 3.1   What these symbols tell us about work.

This pattern is shorthand for the basic "molecule" of work and is a fundamental building block of the maps that appear in this book, in particular the cross-functional process map (swimlane diagram) and flowchart. These I-P-O components are the most prevalent work components that appear in these two types of maps. They often appear as parts of an interconnected set that represents a series of logically interrelated activities within a workflow.

The Map Is Not the Territory (It Is a Model of the Territory)

Here are some other important things about work that may not appear on a map (Figure 3.2).

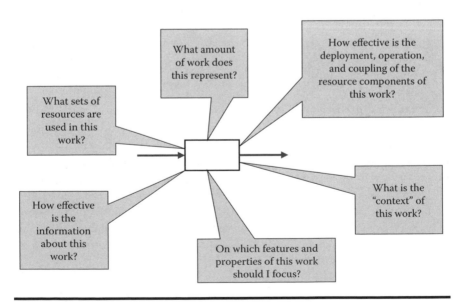

Figure 3.2   What this symbol doesn't tell us about work.

Ever use a road map to plan a route? Then you start driving along the route and find out that there are characteristics and conditions that you wish you had known about before you ran into them, sometimes literally, such as potholes, construction, and traffic delays? The same thing happens when you use a process map to depict work.

Here are some key points about (process) maps to keep in mind:

1. No matter what type of map you use, it will show some components, boundaries, and features of work and not others, and it may not show the current conditions.
2. What matters most is what you see and experience when you observe or perform the work; what goes on the map is, at best, a representation of something you thought was significant enough to draw a visual representation to show others.
3. As such, one of the main reasons to create a map is to create shared understanding of the actual work, preferably among those who perform the actual work.
4. Maps are a means to some other work-related end.

New Types of Maps May Come and Go, but the Work They Represent Will Remain

As I write this, I find that many improvement practitioners are using a value stream map (VSM), also known as a material and information flow diagram. Because I routinely keep current with developments in my field, I was surprised that I had not encountered this map sooner. The reason for this was straightforward.

The value stream map originated as part of the Toyota Production System where it is known as a material and information flow diagram. Initially, it was used mainly in manufacturing settings (hence, the name), though it is increasingly being used outside of manufacturing.

Because I've spent the past 25 years improving knowledge work, i.e., business and transactional processes outside of manufacturing, I hadn't come across it until a few years ago.

Being both tool agnostic and innately curious, I've compared and contrasted this type of workflow model to a swimlane diagram. If you are curious as well, I've posted materials related to VSM on my Web site: www.thebottomlinegroup.com. There, you will find a draft document on value stream maps (similar to those I've written for the three maps I've included in this book).

Whenever you encounter any type of (process) map, especially for the first time, take a few minutes and answer the following questions:

1. What does this map tell me about the work that it represents?
2. What is it emphasizing or highlighting regarding the work?
3. How does this "view" of the work help me better understand that work?
4. In this specific situation, what is the purpose for using this type of map?
5. Is there a good fit between the type of map you are looking at and the purpose (reasons why) you are looking at it?
6. How does this map show work boundaries?
7. Which features of the work does it show and with what symbols and conventions?
8. What work components does the map show?
9. Which properties of the work does it show?
10. How does it show those properties?
11. What *doesn't* the map show that may be important to the purpose you have in mind?
12. What is the "context" of the work that the map shows?
    a. Where does this work fit in with other work of the organization?
    b. Is it a portion of the main workflow of the enterprise?
    c. If not, where in relation to the main workflow does this work occur?
        i. Does it connect directly to it?
            A. If not, how far removed is it from the main workflow?
            B. What is the purpose of this work?
            C. To which workflow does this work contribute?
            D. For which customer or stakeholder is this work required?

This should help you make sense of the map. Better yet, it will add to your knowledge of the work the map represents.

Chapter 4

Relationship Maps

What Is a Relationship Map?

A **relationship map** (Figure 4.1) visually depicts the "parts" of an **organization**, and the *internal* or *external* **supplier–customer relationships** among those parts. It follows a general left to right (resource conversion or *throughput*) sequence. This sequence is represented by the same three components: Supplier, Organization, and Customer; think of this set as the default pattern or "template" for this type of map.

The relationship map helps you view work at the Organization level, thus it does not explicitly show work activities. Rather, it shows the input/output connections among selected parts of the Organization. (The rectangle symbol represents a "part" of an organization; think of a "part" as a "bucket" of resources and activities that becomes a building block of organization structure, such as a department, function, team, project, etc.)

Why Use This Type of Map?

1. Show what the organization "takes in" (resource *inputs*) and what it produces, (transformed resources or *outputs*) i.e. its *items*, products, or services.
2. Show the *component* "parts" that make up the "organization whole" *associated with a specific item*.
3. Highlight what each part *contributes* (which inputs and outputs are linked to which parts of the organization).

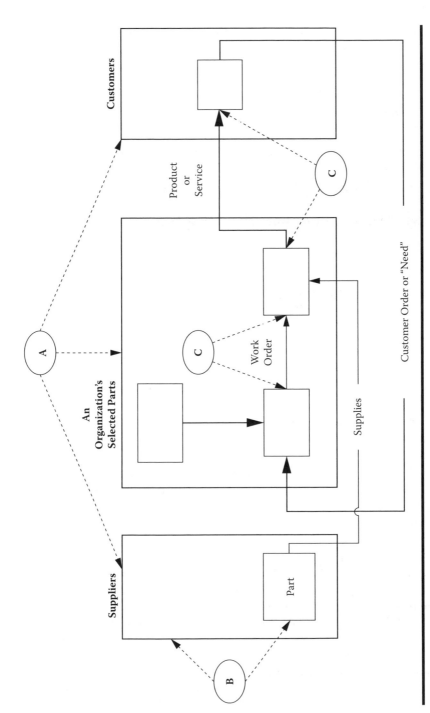

Figure 4.1   Relationship map—Key features: (A) Supplier–organization–customer components, (B) part/whole relationships, (C) supplier–customer relationships.

4. Make selected internal and external supplier-customer relationships visible.
5. Illustrate the organizational boundaries that work must pass through as value is created, i.e. the handoffs.
6. Provide context of work; help orient employees, suppliers, or other stakeholders so they understand how their work "fits in" to the work of the organization.
7. Highlight the parts and connections that are affected by a specific strategy, initiative, or proposed organizational change.

Here are the symbols for this type of map and what each means (Figure 4.2 and Figure 4.3).

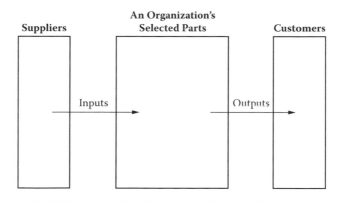

Figure 4.2   The basic relationship map template.

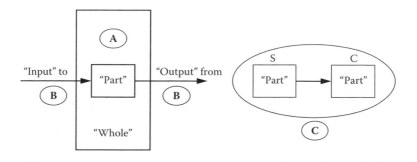

Figure 4.3   Relationship map symbols for (A) part/whole relationship, (B) input/output, (C) supplier–customer (S-C) relationship.

How to Create a Relationship Map

I use relationship maps to identify the "affected parts" of an Organization associated with one of two views of work. I've included procedures to do both, beginning on the next page.

View 1: Order to Delivery ("Why the <u>Business</u> Is Here")

The first procedure highlights the (parts involved with) "Order to Delivery" (OTD) sequence of work, i.e. the primary value-creating work of any Organization. As such, OTD provides the customer value context within which to view work. I discuss this in "reasons to map a process, part 1" of Chapter 3.

I'd recommend that you limit your focus to a single item (product or service) and customer initially. If you start with the main item and the main customer for that item, this should help you understand the general pattern for other similar items and customers as well.

Note: Prior to using this procedure for the first time, you may find it helpful to take a quick peek at the complete step-by step relationship map example for Phil's Quick Lube that appears in the Appendix.

View 2: How Does This *Part "Fit in?"* ("You Are Here")

The second procedure highlights how *any one "part"* of an Organization (that does not appear in the Order to Delivery view) "fits in," and connects with, those parts of the Organization to which it *directly* contributes (Table 4.1, Figure 4.4 to Figure 4.6).

Both procedures assume you are using a group facilitation method to obtain the knowledge needed to create the map. The circled numbers in the figures correspond to the <u>number of the procedure step</u>.

Table 4.1   How to Create a Relationship Map that provides the "Organization View" of Order to Delivery

Step	Action	Fig.
A. Create workspaces and templates		4.4
1	Place a large (at least 3 ft. × 6 ft.) piece of paper on a wall or flat surface	4.7
2	Outline two "workspaces" on the paper	4.7
3	Create a S-C template and place it in "workspace 1"	4.8
4	Create a "basic relationship map" template and place it in "workspace 2"	4.9
B. Define supplier–customer relationships (workspace 1)		4.5
5	Define the **external** supplier–customer relationships *first,* starting with the **external customer**	4.10
6	Define the **external** supplier–customer relationships, starting with the **external supplier**	4.11
7	Define the <u>internal</u> supplier–customer relationships	4.12
C. Create relationship map (workspace 2)		4.6
8	Draw each *unique* part from the S-C template in the corresponding portion of the relationship map template	4.13
9	Draw and label the inputs and outputs to reflect the **connections among the parts as a whole**	4.14
	Start with the external customer connections first	4.14
	Then the external supplier connections	4.15
	And, finally, the internal connections	4.16

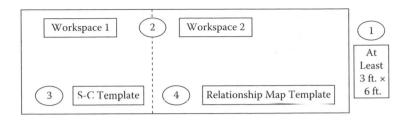

Figure 4.4   Create workspaces and templates.

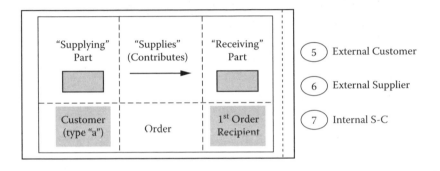

Figure 4.5   Define supplier-customer relationships.

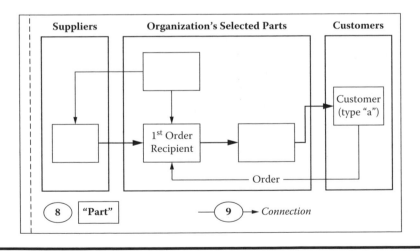

Figure 4.6   Create a relationship map.

1. Place a large (at least 3' × 6") piece of paper on a wall or flat surface (Figure 4.7).
2. Outline two "workspaces" on the paper (Figure 4.7).

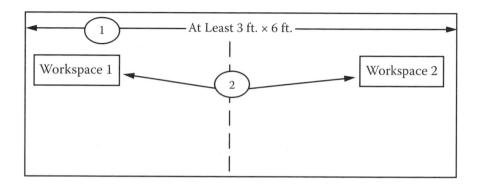

Figure 4.7 Paper on wall with two workspaces.

3. Create a S-C template and place it in "workspace 1" (Figure 4.8).

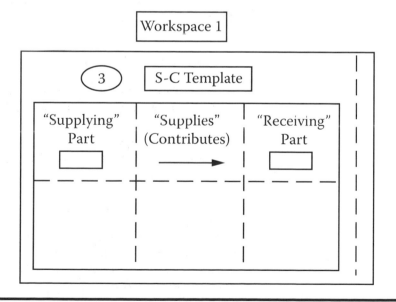

Figure 4.8 Supplier-customer template in workspace 1.

4. Create a "basic relationship map" template and place it in "workspace 2" (Figure 4.9).

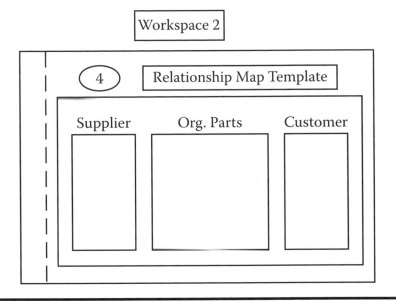

Figure 4.9   Relationship map template in workspace 1.

Steps 5, 6, and 7 make use of the S-C Template and sticky notes

5. Define the external supplier-customer relationships first, starting with the external customer. This will give you the Customer "touch points" (Figure 4.10).
   a.   Pick a single (type of) external customer for a specific item.
   b.   Determine what the customer provides the organization, and what the organization provides to the customer.
      •   Who is the Customer?
      •   What does the Organization first receive from the customer?
      •   What part of the Organization first receives that item?
      •   What else does the Organization receive from the customer, with respect to the first item?"
      •   Which part of the Organization first receives that item?
      •   What does the Organization provide to that customer?
      •   What part of the organization provides that item?

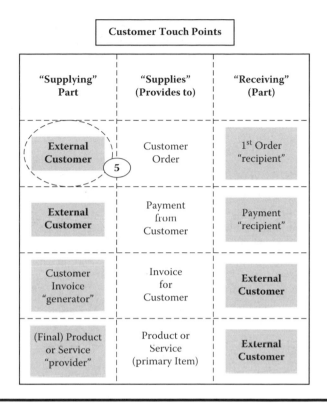

"Supplying" Part	"Supplies" (Provides to)	"Receiving" (Part)
External **Customer**	Customer Order	1st Order "recipient"
External **Customer**	Payment from Customer	Payment "recipient"
Customer Invoice "generator"	Invoice for Customer	**External** **Customer**
(Final) Product or Service "provider"	Product or Service (primary Item)	**External** **Customer**

Customer Touch Points

Figure 4.10 Typical external supplier–customer relationships for Order to Delivery.

6. Define the **external** supplier–customer relationships, starting with the **external supplier.** This will help you identify the supply chain (Figure 4.11).
   a. For the **same main item**, pick a single (type of) supplier associated with that item.
   b. Determine what the supplier provides the organization, and what the organization provides to the supplier.
      i. Who is the supplier?
      ii. What does the organization *first receive* from the supplier?
      iii. What part of the organization *first receives* that item?
      iv. What else does the organization *receive* from the supplier, with respect to the first item?
      v. Which part of the organization first receives *that* item?
      vi. What does the organization *provide* to that supplier?
      vii. What part of the organization *provides that* item?

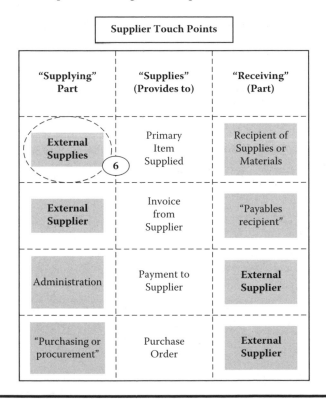

Figure 4.11 Typical external supplier–customer relationships for Order to Delivery.

Steps 5 and 6 identify the most upstream and most downstream parts of the organization directly involved with Order to Delivery. Step 7 determines what happens in between (the middle of the "stream").

7. Define the *internal* supplier–customer relationships (Figure 4.12).
    a. Starting with the first "order recipient," what happens next?
    b. Which part of the organization is involved?
    c. Then, what happens? And so forth, until you reach the most downstream part (the last part of the organization before the item reaches the external customer)?

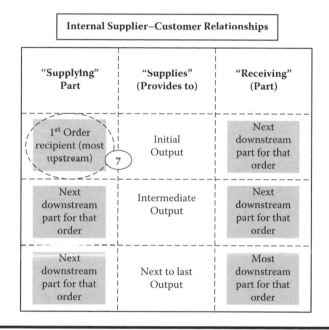

Figure 4.12 Typical *internal* supplier–customer relationships for Order to Delivery.

8. Draw each *unique* part from the S-C template in the corresponding portion of the relationship map template (Figure 4.13).

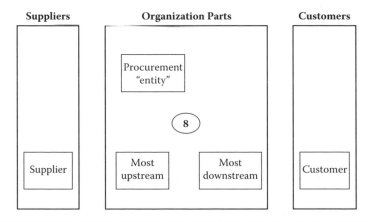

Figure 4.13   Unique organization parts arranged in general Order to Delivery sequence.

9. Draw and label the inputs and outputs to reflect the **connections among the parts as a whole**.
   a. External customer (Figure 4.14)
   b. External supplier (Figure 4.15
   c. Internal connections (Figure 4.16)

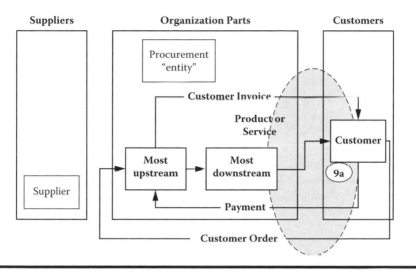

Figure 4.14 External customer touch points highlighted in typical Order to Delivery sequence.

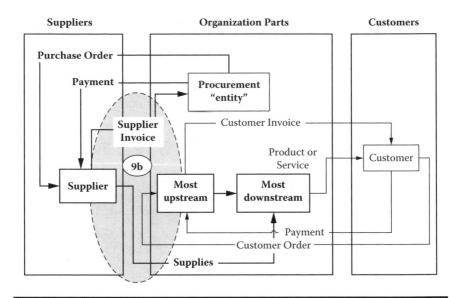

Figure 4.15 External supplier touch points highlighted in typical Order to Delivery sequence.

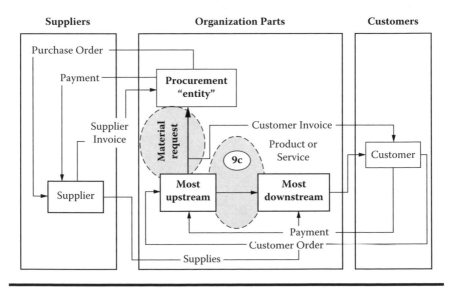

Figure 4.16 Internal supplier–customer relationships highlighted in typical Order to Delivery sequence.

Here is the completed relationship map (Figure 4.17).

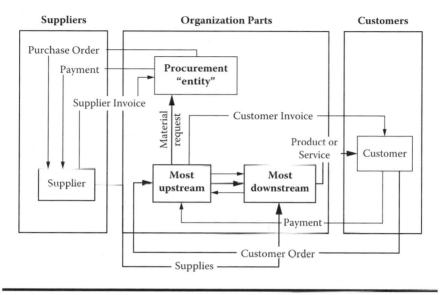

Figure 4.17   Relationship map of typical Order to Delivery components.

Table 4.2   How to Create a Relationship Map ("Organization view" of Supplier-Customer Relationships for "Your Part"

Step	Step	Fig.
A. Create workspaces and templates		4.18
1	Place a large (at least 3 ft. × 6 ft.) piece of paper on a wall or flat surface	4.21
2	Outline two "workspaces" on the paper	4.21
3	Create a S-C template and place it in "workspace 1"	4.22
4	Create a "basic relationship map" template and place it in "workspace 2"	4.23
B. Define supplier–customer relationships (workspace 1)		4.19
5	In the column "**your part,**" <u>list</u> the name of your part of the organization	4.24
6	In the column **"Supplies to,"** <u>list</u> the major **output(s)** of "your part"	4.25
7	In the column **"This Part, as your** *Customer*,**"** <u>list</u> the *immediate* **customer(s)** for each unique output	4.26
8	In the column **"Provides to,"** <u>list</u> the major **input(s)** that "your part" requires to produce each output	4.27
9	In the column "**This Part as Your** *Supplier*,**"** <u>list</u> from where each input comes from	4.28
C. Create relationship map (workspace 2)		4.20
10	Draw each part from the S-C template in the corresponding portion of the relationship map	4.29
11	Draw and label the inputs and outputs to reflect the **connections among the parts as a whole**	4.30

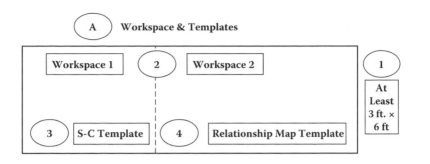

Figure 4.18   Create workspaces and templates.

Steps 5, 6, 7, 8, and 9 use a S-C Template and sticky notes (Figure 4.19).

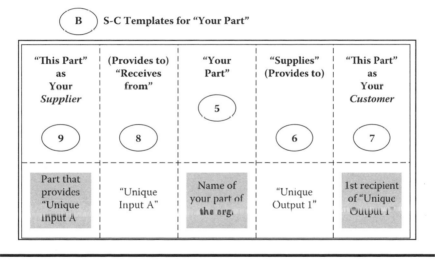

Figure 4.19   Define supplier-customer relationship.

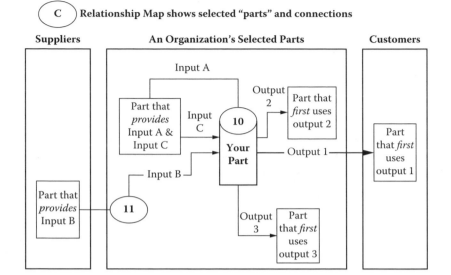

Figure 4.20 Create relationship map.

1. Place a large (at least 3' × 6") piece of paper on a wall or flat surface (Figure 4.21).
2. Outline two "workspaces" on the paper (Figure 4.21).

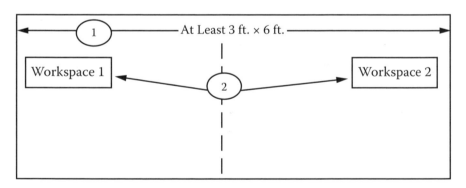

Figure 4.21 Paper on wall with two workspaces.

3. Create a S-C template and place it in "workspace 1" (Figure 4.22).

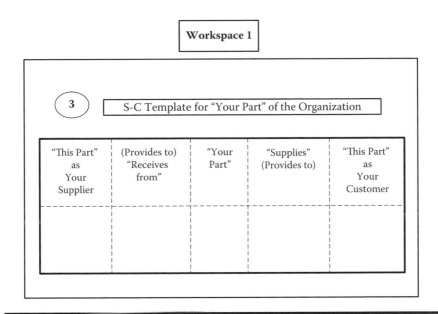

Figure 4.22   Supplier-customer template in workspace 1.

4. Create a "basic relationship map" template and place it in "workspace 2" (Figure 4.23).

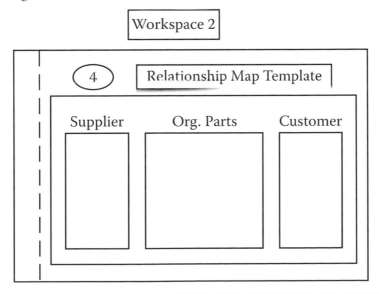

Figure 4.23   Relationship map template in workspace 2.

5. In the column "**Your Part**," <u>list</u> the name of your part of the organization (Figure 4.24).

S-C Template for "Your Part" of the Organization				
"This Part" as Your *Suppliers*	(Provides to) "Receives from"	"**Your Part**" ⑤	"Supplies" (Provides to)	"This Part" as Your *Customer*
		Name of your part of the org.		

Figure 4.24 Supplier–customer template containing the name of "Your Part" of the organization.

6. In the column **"Supplies to,"** list the major **output(s)**of "your part" (Figure 4.25).

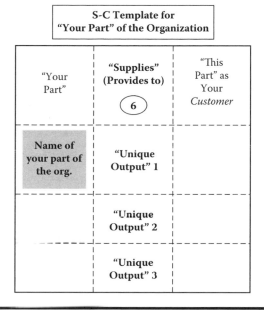

Figure 4.25   Supplier–customer template for "Your Part" of the organization with "Unique Outputs" added.

7. In the column **"This Part, as Your** *Customer***,"** list the *immediate* **customers** for each unique output (Figure 4.26).

S-C Template for "Your Part" of the Organization		
"Your Part"	"Supplies" (Provides to)	"This Part" as Your *Customer* (7)
Name of your part of the org.	"Unique Output" 1	*First* **recipient of "Unique Output 1"**
	"Unique Output" 2	*First* **recipient of "Unique Output 2"**
	"Unique Output" 3	*First* **recipient or "Unique Output 3"**

Figure 4.26   Supplier–customer template for "Your Part" of the organization with *immediate* customers added.

8. In the column **"Provides to,"** list the major **inputs** that "Your Part" requires to produce each output (Figure 4.27).

S-C Template for "Your Part" of the Organization			
(Provides to) "Receives from" ⑧	"Your Part"	"Supplies" (Provides to)	"This Part" as Your *Customer*
"Unique Input" A	Name of your part of the org.	"Unique Output" 1	*First* recipient or "Unique Output 1"
"Unique Input" B		"Unique Output" 2	*First* recipient or "Unique Output 2"
"Unique Input" C		"Unique Output" 3	*First* recipient or "Unique Output 3"

Figure 4.27 Supplier–Customer template for "Your Part" of the organization with *inputs* added.

9. In the column "**This Part as Your** *Supplier*," <u>list</u> where each input comes from (Figure 4.28).

S-C Template for "Your Part" of the Organization				
"This Part" as Your *Suppliers* ⑨	(Provides to) "Receives from"	"Your Part"	"Supplies" (Provides to)	"This Part" as Your *Customer*
Part that provides "Unique Input A"	"Unique Input" 1 For *mapping* purposes, assume it comes form an internal supplier	Name of your part of the org.	"Unique Output" 1 For *mapping* purposes, assume it goes to an external customer	*First* recipient of "Unique Output 1"
Part that provides "Unique Input B"	"Unique Input" B For *mapping* purposes, assume it comes form an external supplier		"Unique Output" 2 For *mapping* purposes, assume it goes to an internal customer	*First* recipient of "Unique Output 2"
Part that provides "Unique Input C"	"Unique Input" C For *mapping* purposes, assume it come form the same internal supplier as "A"		"Unique Output" 3 For *mapping* purposes, assume it goes to different internal customer	*First* recipient of "Unique Output 3"

Figure 4.28 Supplier–customer template for "Your Part" of the organization with *immediate* suppliers added.

10. Draw each part from the S-C template in the corresponding portion of the relationship map template (Figure 4.29).

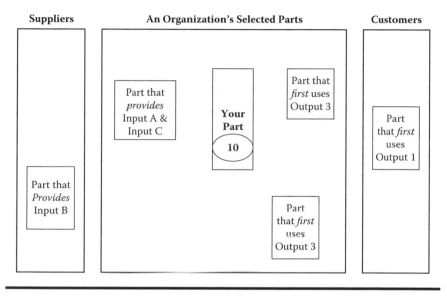

Figure 4.29 Relationship map (partial) for "Your Part" of the organization with *immediate* supplier and customer parts.

11. Draw and label the inputs and outputs to reflect the **connections among the parts as a whole** (Figure 4.30).

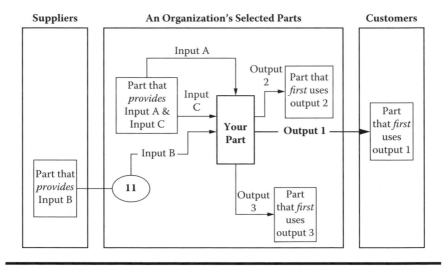

Figure 4.30   Relationship map for "Your Part" of the organization with *immediate* supplier–customer relationships shown (output and connections added).

Relationship Map Interview

Overview

The following scene takes place in the office of Phil Greene, the owner of Phil's Quick Lube. Phil has contracted with Oscar Smith, a process improvement consultant, to help him better understand operations and improve profitability. Oscar is using the one-on-one interview method to generate a relationship map of the garage. Here is a transcript of the interview. The resultant relationship map follows at the end of the interview.

Interview

Oscar: As we discussed, I need your help understanding the big picture of the work done here at your business. In simple terms, what type of work does Phil's Quick Lube provide to your customers?

Phil: We provide preventive maintenance services in these areas: change the oil, maintain or replace battery, replenish "fluids," such as transmission or cooling systems.

Oscar: Anything else?

Phil: Annual vehicle inspections.

Oscar: Which service is your biggest money maker?

Phil: That would be oil changes because of the number we do, not the price.

Oscar: What starts the work related to an oil change?

Phil: We use written service orders for all services. Nothing happens until there is a service order approved by the customer.

Oscar: What part of the business is responsible for obtaining the approved service order from the customer?

Phil: Sales. They work directly with the customer. They talk with the customer to figure out what they need, write the service order, and when the work is done they present the invoice to the customer and collect payment.

Oscar: During an oil change, does Sales have any other forms to complete, besides service orders and invoices?

Phil: Well, they generate material requests and send them to Administration. Administration uses the material request to generate purchase orders for the various supplies we use. They don't do this during each oil change though; they do it once a week.

Oscar: Which part of the business actually changes the oil?

Phil: Service. We have three bays that are designed to do certain work. One does oil changes only. Another can handle battery work or fluid replenishment, and the third is used for annual vehicle inspections because the diagnostic equipment costs a lot and is hard to move.

Oscar: Okay, Sales writes a service order for an oil change. What happens to that Service order next?

Phil: It goes in the job packet, along with the ignition key. The Sales person who prepares the job packet hands it to the next available Service tech for that type of work.

Oscar: What happens to the job packet?

Phil: It stays with the car until the work is done. Then the Service tech hands it to the Sales person who generated it, so they can create the invoice and collect the money from the customer after the work is done.

Oscar: So, in the case of an oil change, when the oil change service tech gets the job packet, what happens?

Phil: The Service tech reads the service order and begins to change the oil in the vehicle.

Oscar: In the oil change bay?

Phil: Yes.

Oscar: How did the vehicle get to the oil change bay?

Phil: After Sales writes the service order, they get the ignition keys from the customer, and move the vehicle to the oil change bay. Then, they put the keys and the service order in the job packet and hand it to the Service tech.

Oscar: What happens to the vehicle after the oil is changed?

Phil: The Service tech moves the vehicle to the pick-up area, removes the keys, and puts the keys and the service order back in the job packet. Then, they return the job packet to the Sales person, like I told you earlier.

Oscar: Thanks. Bear with me, I'm a slow learner. So, now I understand how the vehicle got to the oil change bay so that the oil could be changed. And I can see that after the oil is changed, the vehicle is moved to the pick-up area. Where does the replacement oil come from that you use during the oil change?

Phil: That's why I told you about the material request. We order all our supplies from an auto parts distributor. We send them a PO weekly, they deliver supplies weekly and leave us an invoice. We pay those once a month.

Oscar: Which parts of the organization are involved with supplies and supplier invoices?

Phil: Supplies go to Service. Supplier invoices go to Administration. They also send out the POs and make the monthly payments.

Oscar: We've covered a lot of ground, Phil. Are there any other parts of the business involved with an oil change? If not, let's stop and take a look at what I've drawn so far (Figure 4.31).

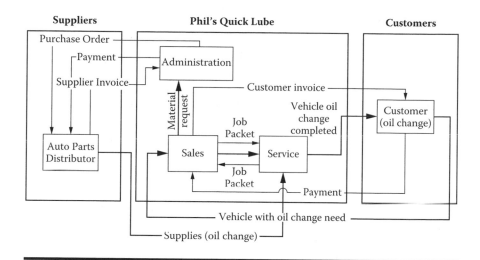

Figure 4.31   Organization view of Phil's Quick Lube oil change shown with a relationship map.

Interpreting Relationship Maps

Relationship maps show how the parts of an organization are "wired" together. They can help you better understand who does what to whom, i.e., what the supplier–customer links are throughout the organization. Every function, department, or team is always a supplier (it produces one or more outputs) and a customer (it receives one or more inputs from somewhere else). A relationship map helps you quickly identify these supplier–customer connections and answer the following questions:

1. Who are the customers for my part of the business?
2. What outputs do they receive from me?
3. Who are the suppliers to my part of the business?
4. What inputs do I receive from them?
5. How does my part of the business fit in with or contribute to the rest of the organization?
   a. Is my part of the business a subset or portion of the main order to delivery workflow of the business?
   b. If not, how does it relate to that workflow?

6. What are the critical internal connections (the handoffs) between my area and the rest of the organization?

A relationship map highlights **part/whol**e relationships and **supplier–customer** relationships.

Here's why part/whole relationships matter. Every business (even Phil's) has some type of order to delivery workflow. This workflow starts and ends with an external customer and encompasses several parts of the business. Once you make these part/whole relationships visible, you know what parts of the organization should be aligned so that they operate as a single, integrated whole *with respect to the flow of the work involved with turning an order into the product or service that the customer receives*. You also know the contribution that each part makes to the whole (end-to-end) workflow.

Supplier–customer relationships generally provide significant opportunities to improve quality, reduce waste, improve flow, and reduce lead time. Where there is a handoff between one part of the organization and another, you should determine whether, and to what extent, the requirements for each input/output are mutually understood (between supplying and receiving organizations) and are being met. You also should assess how well each organizational handoff is being measured or managed.

Interpreting the Relationship Map View of Phil's Quick Lube

How might you interpret the map and information you have gained thus far? Consider the following questions as you refer to Figure 4.31.

1. What are the *boundaries* of the work shown in this map?
   Organization(s)
   - Supplier(s), a set of businesses that provide resources to Phil's
   - Phil's Quick Lube
   - Customer(s), a set of people that purchase services that Phil's offers
2. What *components* of work does this map show?
   - **Parts** (structural components) of the various organizations:
     - Auto parts distributor, of the set of businesses that provide resources to Phil's, this is one related to oil change work
     - Administration, Sales, Service
     - Oil change customer, of the set of customers that purchase services, this is one that purchases an oil change

- **Inputs and outputs** (specific forms of resources associated with the work related to an oil change only)
  - Vehicle (before and after the oil change)
  - Oil change supplies
  - Customer invoice
  - Job packet
  - Payment (from oil change customer)
3. What *features* of work does it show?
  - (Organization) part/whole relationships and supplier–customer relationships (oil change work only)
4. What *properties* of work does it show?
  - Interdependency among structural components associated with an oil change
5. What are the main **external** supplier–customer relationships (Table 4.3)?

Table 4.3 *External* **Supplier-Customer Relationships**

"Supplying" Part	*"Supplies" (Provides to)*	*"Receiving" Part*
Customer (oil change)	Vehicle with need for oil change	Sales
Customer for (oil change)	Payment	Sales
Sales	Invoice	Customer for (oil change)
Service	Vehicle with oil change completed	Customer for (oil change)
Auto Parts Distributor	Supplies related to oil change (oil, oil filter, perhaps?)	Service
Auto Parts Distributor	Invoice for supplies	Administration
Administration	Purchase order for supplies	Auto Parts Distributor
Administration	Payment for supplies	Auto Parts Distributor

6. What are the connections between the parts of the organization (the hand-offs of work from one part of the organization to another) (Table 4.4)?

Table 4.4 *Internal* **Supplier-Customer Relationships**

"Supplying" Part	*"Supplies" (Provides to)*	*"Receiving"* Part
Sales	Vehicle with need for oil change	Service
Sales	Job packet (includes service order and ignition keys)	Service
Sales	Material requests	Administration
Service	Job packet (includes service order and ignition keys)	Sales

7. Are you able to trace the flow of major inputs and outputs as they move throughout the business along the Order to Delivery path? The Supply Path?

Order to Delivery Path: Vehicle leads to Service order, which along with ignition keys, go in Job packet. Job packet and vehicle, along with supplies, are used to change the oil in the oil change bay. Then, vehicle and job packet leave the oil change bay. Vehicle goes to pick-up area. Job packet used to create customer invoice, which leads to payment from the customer.

Supply Path: The Supply path starts with material requests that lead to purchase orders, which lead to supplies and an invoice from the auto parts distributor (supplier). Supplies are delivered to the oil change bay and the invoice goes to Administration, which sends a payment to the auto parts distributor.

8. What are the requirements associated with handoffs? (The interview does not provide us with this information.)
9. Do any other questions come to mind based on the information provided in the interview or from reviewing the completed map? Possibilities include:

■ What happens to the payment collected by Sales from the Customer?
■ Do the three bays work with each other in any way?

- Do they share information?
- What information is needed on a work order for work to begin?
- How do you know that the work each bay performs is correct?
- Are there any issues or opportunities related to the handoffs?

Always walk the path that the work *actually* follows. Observe what happens. (See tips for more information on this.) Maps begin as rough drafts. Then, depending on the methods used to gain the knowledge needed to create the map, and, in light of the goals for creating it in the first place, you make adjustments, review it with others, or move on having learned all that you need to make changes.

Chapter 5

Cross-Functional Process Map (aka Swimlane Diagram)

What Is a Cross-Functional Process Map or Swimlane Diagram?

A **cross-functional process** map (CFPM) illustrates **workflow** in organizations (Figure 5.1). A workflow consists of a set and series of interrelated work activities that follow a distinct path as work inputs (resources) get transformed into outputs (items) that customers value. The name, **cross-functional process map**, means the *whole work process "crosses" several functions*.

It also is called a **swimlane diagram** because the pattern of the horizontal bands is similar to the lanes of an Olympic swimming pool (as seen from *above* the pool).

Whereas the *relationship* map only shows the parts of an organization, the cross-functional process map shows the **work** that takes place in each **part**. *Note that the rectangles that represent* **organizational "parts"** *on a relationship map become horizontal bands or "swimlanes" on the CFPM.*

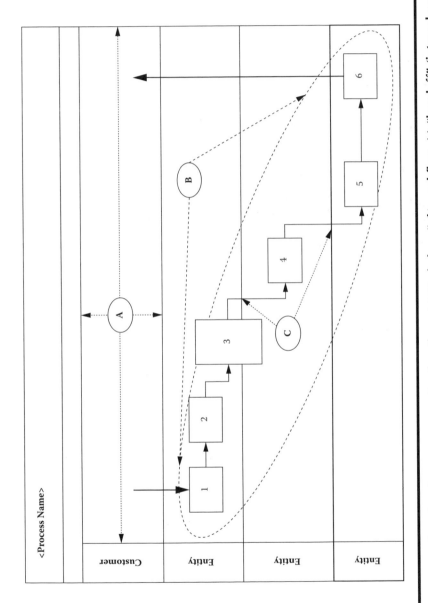

Figure 5.1 Cross-functional process map—Key functions: (a) "Swimlane," (b) workflow, (c) "handoff" (internal supplier–customer (S-C) relationship.

Why Use This Type of Map?

1. Show the boundaries (beginning and end) and an entire workflow at a glance
2. Highlight customer touch points
3. Simultaneously show work and where in the organization that work takes place
4. Make the supplier–customer relationships that exist throughout the process visible
5. Illustrate the organizational handoffs
6. Identify patterns in the workflow (serial, collaborative, parallel, or a combination)

Here are several symbols and conventions for this type of map and what each means (Figure 5.2).

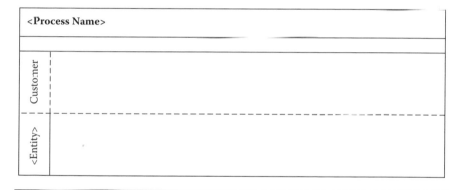

Figure 5.2 **Basic template for swimlane diagram showing default position for the customer.**

I always designate and include the customer as the topmost swimlane. This immediately provides one very important context for the work represented on the map. The work may or may not directly relate to or touch the customer.

In what order should multiple swimlanes be sequenced? One guideline is to order them according to their interaction with the customer. A direct, frequent interaction would be closest to the customer swimlane. Less frequent, or indirect, would be farther away. The more swimlanes there are between the customer and the work shown on the map, the more closely that work should be assessed with respect to customer value.

A Closer Look at a Swimlane

Swimlanes have two key elements (Figure 5.3).

The dotted line (a) represents the boundary of the entity.

The name of the entity (b) appears in the leftmost portion of the swimlane.

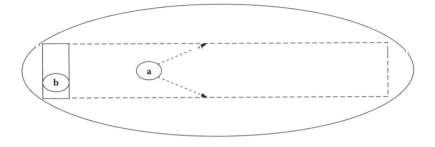

Figure 5.3 Symbols for (a) swimlane boundaries and (b) name of responsible entity.

Mapping Conventions

1. Use a "box" to show the activities within a workflow or process. Shade the box if you have a separate map or flowchart of this activity (Figure 5.4).

Figure 5.4 Symbols for activity.

2. Draw a line with an arrow to show an input or an output associated with each activity. Label the inputs and outputs. This helps with subsequent interpretation. The input should be the resource that the activity transforms. You should be able to see the transformation, and the value-creating work of an activity reflected in the progression of outputs throughout the workflow. Note that the direction of the arrow is also the direction of the flow of work (Figure 5.5).

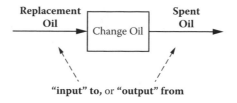

Figure 5.5   Symbols for inputs and outputs.

3. Keep general left-to-right sequence of converting inputs into outputs (Figure 5.6).

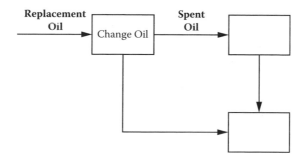

Figure 5.6   General left-to-right "conversion" sequence.

4. Arrows representing inputs or outputs should pass over or under one another, rather than intersect (Figure 5.7).

Figure 5.7   Inputs and outputs pass over or under one another.

5. Use the diamond symbol to indicate a decision (alternate branches and paths of flow). Often there are more than two options so label all the branches (Figure 5.8).

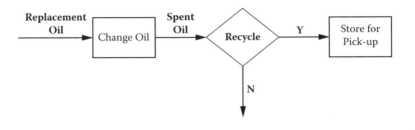

Figure 5.8 Symbol for decision with two branches.

6. Draw horizontal bands (swimlanes) to represent the "entity" that does the work. Inputs and outputs pass through these bands (Figure 5.9).

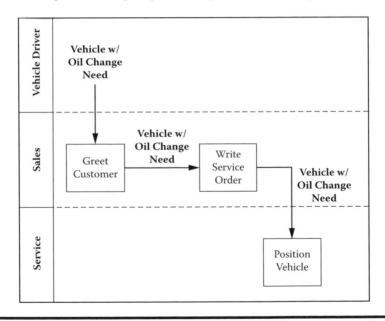

Figure 5.9 Swimlane diagram showing three entities: Vehicle Drive, Sales, and Service.

An entity may be a job title or role, a function or department, a specific IT system, and in general, anything that holds the work. The dotted lines of swimlanes represent a "shared boundary, or *interface*." When an input or output crosses a boundary it is called a "handoff"(between the two entities). Handoffs are rarely synchronized, and active management of boundaries is seldom the default condition.

7. When several entities jointly perform the *same* activity, draw the box so that it includes all the entities involved (Figure 5.10). Solid lines show shared involvement or *collaboration*. Dotted lines show that one or more entities are *not* involved with the activity.

Here, customer history is reviewed by entities (a), (b), and (c).

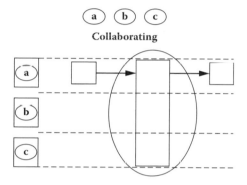

Figure 5.10 **Pattern of a collaborative activity between (a), (b), and (c).**

Next, customer history is reviewed by (a) and (c); entity (b) is not involved (Figure 5.11).

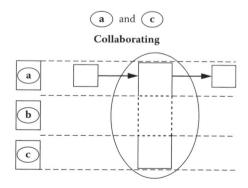

Figure 5.11 **Pattern of a collaborative activity between (a) and (c).**

8. Split (subdivide) the band if you want to show a subset of similar work within the same entity (Figure 5.12).

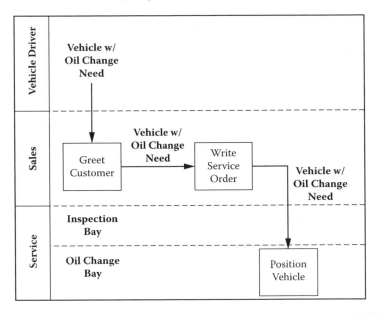

Figure 5.12   Swimlane diagram with "split band" showing two distinct bays in the Service Department.

9. Often, you may discover that two different activities (performed by different entities) may occur at roughly the same time. These are *parallel* activities (Figure 5.13).

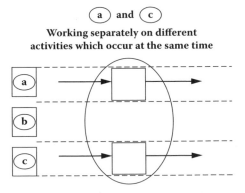

Figure 5.13   Pattern of two parallel activities.

10. This is a *serial* workflow pattern. It occurs regularly in knowledge work (Figure 5.14).

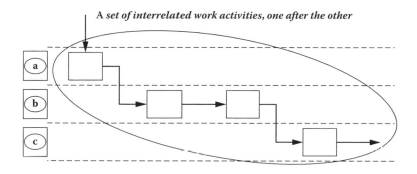

Figure 5.14   Workflow with a "serial" pattern.

11. This is the pattern of *internal* supplier–customer relationships (Figure 5.15).

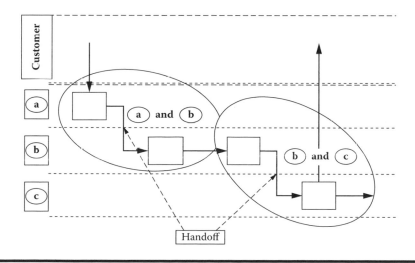

Figure 5.15   Internal supplier–customer relationships involve a handoff from one internal entity to another internal entity.

12. This is the pattern of *external* supplier–customer relationships (Figure 5.16).

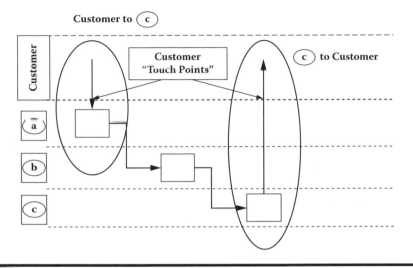

Figure 5.16   External supplier–customer relationships involve an input or output that directly connects the customer with some part of the organization.

How to Create a Cross-Functional Process Map

1. Place a large (at least 3 ft. × 6 ft.) piece of paper on a wall or flat surface (Figure 5.17).
2. Draw one horizontal band for each "responsible entity" involved in the process. Bands may be used to represent organization parts or functions, roles, job titles, IT systems, even in-boxes, or other *places where work accumulates.*
3. Label the swimlanes from the top, begining with the external customer followed by the entities closest to the customer.

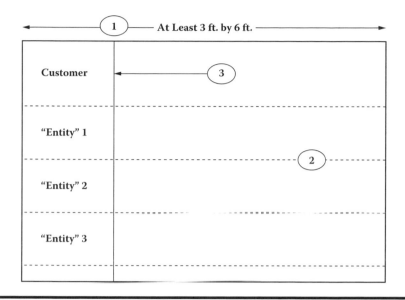

Figure 5.17   Workspace used to create a swimlane diagram showing swimlane boundaries with labels, and with the customer swimlane at the top.

4. Ask each group member to write the activities that make up his/her portion of the process on Post-it® notes (one activity per note), and place the Post-it notes on the *mapping paper* (Figure 5.18).

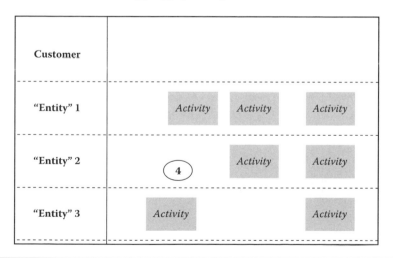

Figure 5.18   Swimlane diagram (partial); activities added using Post-it notes.

5. Arrange the Post-its so that the group is satisfied that the map reflects the item flow (Figure 5.19).

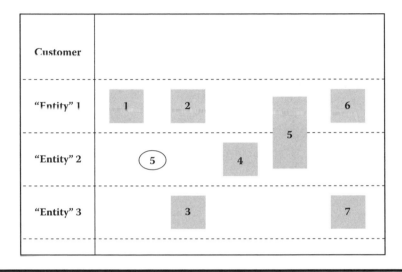

Figure 5.19   Swimlane diagram (partial); activities sequenced using Post-it notes.

6. Add and label all inputs and outputs (Figure 5.20).

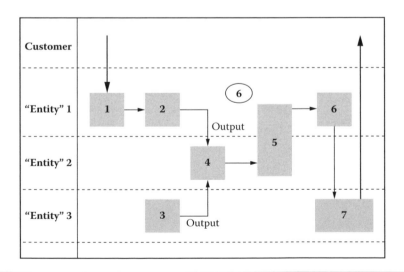

Figure 5.20   Swimlane diagram (partial); outputs and connections added and labeled using Post-it notes.

7. Use application software to document the map (Figure 5.21). Take digital picture(s) of the map on the wall (especially if you want to chronicle its development).

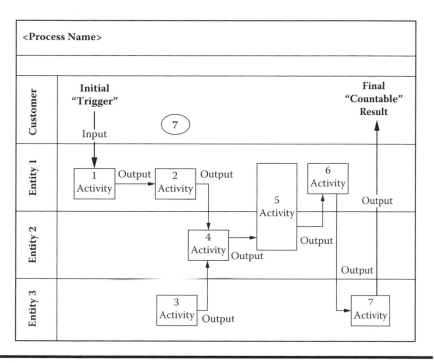

Figure 5.21   Swimlane diagram using "mapping" software.

Cross-Functional Process Map Interview

Overview

This is a continuation of the discussion between Phil Greene and Oscar Smith that began in Chapter 4. There have been no adjustments or changes to the relationship map (Figure 4.17) resulting from that conversation.

Script

Oscar: Let's take a closer look at the work associated with an oil change. Walk me through the work beginning with the arrival of a customer.

Phil: Someone from Sales greets the customer, discusses the work to be done, writes a service order, and confirms with the customer the work to be done.

Oscar: What happens next?

Phil: Sales gives the service order to the next available oil change Service tech, who reviews it and prepares to start the job.

Oscar: What does the Service technician do?

Phil: He takes the keys out of the job packet, locates the customer's car, and moves it to the oil change bay. Then, he prepares the vehicle for an oil change. Next, he changes the oil. Then, he places a reminder sticker on the front windshield of the car, and does a quality check. Once he confirms that everything is okay, he moves the car to the pick-up area, and notifies Sales that the job is complete. At this point, he returns the job packet to the Sales person who wrote the service order.

Oscar: Once the Service technician notifies Sales, they prepare the bill for the customer and collect payment, right?

Phil: Right.

Oscar: Can you think of anything else that takes place as part of an oil change?

Phil: Not right now. I think we've about covered it.

Oscar: Let's take a look at the map of the oil change work (Figure 5.22).

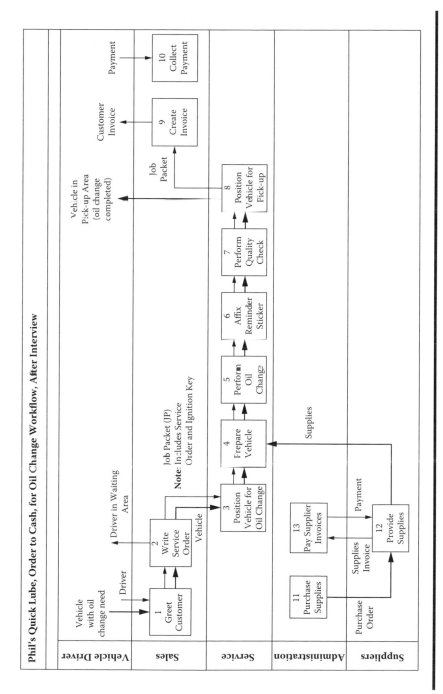

Figure 5.22 Swimlane diagram of Phil's Quick Lube, order to cash, for oil change workflow, after interview.

Interpreting Cross-Functional Process Maps

Cross-functional process maps (swimlane diagrams) show workflow *boundaries* and highlight selected components *relevant* to that workflow. Whereas *relationship* maps focus more on the links between the structural "parts" that make up a business, **cross-functional process maps show** *what takes place within* those parts.

Cross-functional process maps answer the questions:

- Where does the workflow *begin* and *end* (what are the workflow *boundaries*)
- What *set* of activities produce the main output of (the *item* that exits) this workflow?
- What is the order in which the activities are performed?
- What are the inputs required and the outputs produced at each activity?
- Is the value-creating transformation from **input** to *item*, readily apparent?
- What "triggers" the workflow to begin?
- What is the countable result that exits the workflow?
- Which entities are responsible for performing each activity?
- What handoffs or interfaces exist between entities?
- Where in the workflow do these occur?
- What is the workflow "pattern?"

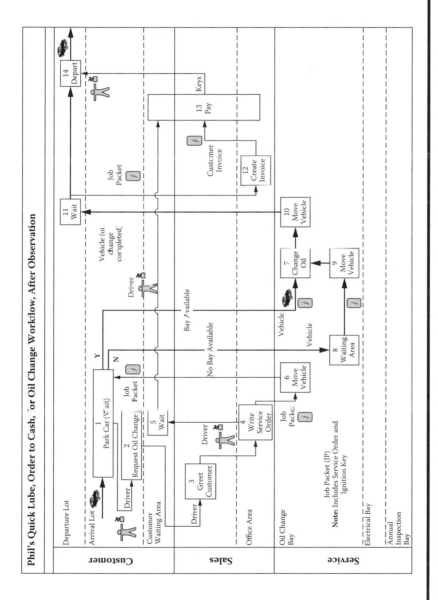

Figure 5.23   **Phil's Quick Lube Order to Cash for an oil change workflow (after observation of work).**

Interpreting the Cross-Functional Process Map of Phil's Quick Lube

I've included two versions of a cross-functional process map associated with this work. The first version (Figure 5.22) is based on the *interview* only. The second version (Figure 5.23) is based on the interview *plus* observation of the work. I used the second version for this interpretation.

1. What are the *boundaries* of the work shown in this map?
   - Customer parks car upon arrival; customer drives off after paying. (Order to cash for an oil change only.)
2. What *set* of activities produce the main output of (the *item* that exits) this workflow?
   - Activities 1–14 in Figure 5.23. Note that this map does not include the supply-related workflow (activities 11–13 in Figure 5.22).
3. What is the order in which the activities are performed? (1–14).
4. What are the inputs required and the outputs produced at each activity? See labels on the map and also the following discussion.
5. Is the value-creating transformation from <u>input</u> to *item*, readily apparent?
   - There are four *work item* flows to consider:
     1. Customer
     2. Vehicle
     3. Information
     4. Supplies

Please refer to Figure 5.23. I've used icons to highlight the flow of the customer, the vehicle, and information. The supplies do not show up in this map.

The Flow of the Customer

The *presence of a Customer and vehicle located in the arrival area* "triggers" the workflow. After talking to a Sales person, the Customer goes to the waiting area- and waits until the work is completed, the vehicle is parked in the pick up area, and an invoice is created. Once the Customer pays the invoice in the Office area, they get the key, find their car in the pick up area, and leave.

The Flow of the Vehicle

The vehicle starts in the arrival area. It waits until it is moved to the oil change bay, or to an adjacent parking area next to the oil change bay if the bay is currently occupied, where it waits until the bay is empty.

After the oil has been changed, the vehicle is moved to the pick-up area where it waits until the invoice has been paid and the keys are returned to the customer.

The Flow of Information

When the Sales person greets the customer, he/she gathers information such as oil type and brand preference from the Customer. This information is entered into a pc that generates the service order that is prepared and printed out in the Office. The service order and the ignition key are placed in a job packet. The job packet triggers the movement of the vehicle from now on. The job packet leaves the office and goes to the arrival parking area. It moves from there to the oil change bay. Here it triggers the oil change. Information in the service order is used to select the oil, relevant supplies, and the procedure to use for the oil change. After the oil has been changed, the job packet leaves the oil change bay and accompanies the Vehicle to the pick up area. Then the job packet moves to the office area where it is used to create the customer invoice, which leads to payment from the customer.

The Flow of Supplies

Oil change supplies are held in inventory in a storage area within the oil change bay. Unlike the above three flows that are all triggered by each individual vehicle, the replenishment of supplies is triggered by usage levels. It is a separate workflow; the timing of which is related to the mix and volume of oil changes.

6. What "triggers" the workflow to begin?
   - The *presence* of a Customer and vehicle located in the arrival area
7. What is the countable result that exits the workflow?
   - Oil changes completed and paid for
8. Which entities are responsible for performing each activity?
   - Customer (vehicle driver) 1,2,5,11,14
   - Sales associate 3,4,12,13
   - Service technician 6,7,8,9,10
9. What handoffs or interfaces exist between entities?

"Supplying" Part	"Supplies" (Provides to)	"Receiving" Part
Sales	Vehicle with need for oil change	Service
Sales	Job packet (includes service order and ignition keys)	Service
Service	Job packet (includes service order and ignition keys)	Sales

10. Where in the workflow do these occur?
    - 4-6; 10-11; 11-12; 13-14
11. What is the workflow "pattern?"
    - Serial (one activity after another) with a collaborative activity (payment) at the end.

Some additional information the map contains:

1. What *components* of work does this map show?
    - Activities, main input (vehicle needing oil change), final item (vehicle with the oil changed), other related inputs, outputs (the vehicle driver, invoice, car keys, payment, etc.)
    - Entities: Customer, Sales, Service
    - Facilities (arrival and departure parking areas, customer waiting area, office, oil change, electrical, and annual inspection service bays)
2. What *features* of work does it show?
    - Part/whole workflow relationships, supplier-customer relationships, organization handoffs, triggers
3. What *properties* of work does it show?
    - Interdependency
    - Flow
    - Value, Waste
4. What are the main **external** supplier-customer relationships?

"Supplying" Part	*"Supplies"* *(Provides to)*	*"Receiving" Part*
Customer (oil change)	Vehicle with need for oil change	Sales
Customer for (oil change)	Payment	Sales
Sales	Invoice	Customer for (oil change)
Sales	Ignition keys	Customer for (oil change)
Service	Vehicle with oil change completed	Customer for (oil change)

Chapter 6

Flowchart

What Is a Flowchart?

A **flowchart** is a graphic representation (Figure 6.1) of the sequence of **activities** used to create, produce, or provide a specific, unique output.

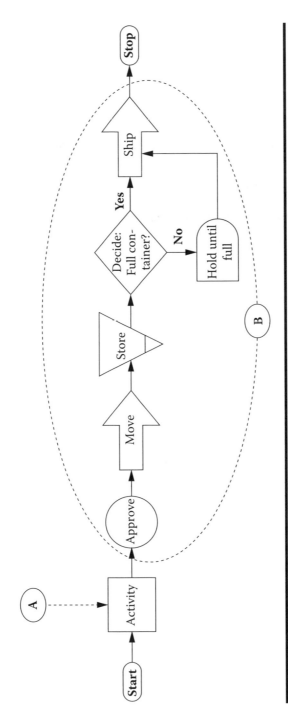

Figure 6.1 Flowchart: (a) Value-creating activity, (b) nonvalue-creating activities.

Why Use This Type of Map?

1. "Drill down" within a subset, or portion of a larger process, to show the "ground -truth" reality of what actually happens.
2. Distinguish between value-creating and nonvalue-creating activity.
3. Make types of waste in the nonvalue-creating activity visible, such as delays, storage, batching, movement, inspection, approval, rework, etc.

Typical flowchart symbols (Figure 6.2).

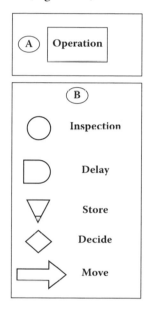

Figure 6.2   Flowchart symbols for (a) value-creating activity and (b) nonvalue-creating activities.

How to Create a Flowchart

1. Define the boundaries of the work (Figure 6.3).

Figure 6.3   Symbols for boundaries.

2. Keep the flow of the work from left to right **or** top to bottom (Figure 6.4).

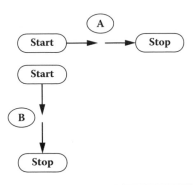

Figure 6.4   Keep the flow (a) left to right or (b) top to bottom.

3. Build intelligence into your flowcharts; make use of all applicable symbols (Figure 6.5).

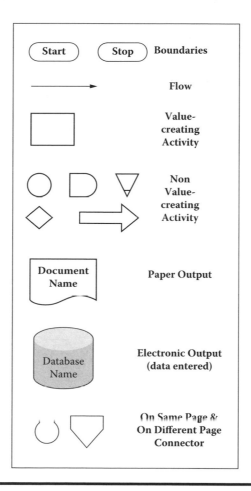

Figure 6.5   Use meaningful symbols.

4. Keep the symbols about the same distance from one another (Figure 6.6).

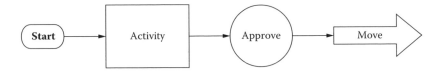

Figure 6.6   Similar distance between symbols.

5. Avoid crossing lines (Figure 6.7).

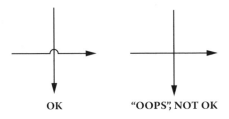

Figure 6.7   Flow should pass over and under.

6. Make sure the branches of your decision symbols are labeled (Figure 6.8).

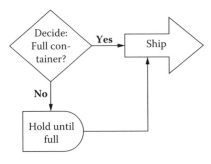

Figure 6.8   Decision branches labeled Yes or No.

7. Identify the output of the workflow (Figure 6.9).

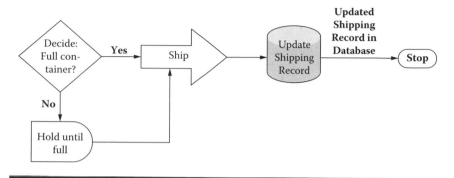

Figure 6.9   Identify the output.

Flowchart

Overview

The following scene takes place in the office of Phil Greene, the owner of Phil's Quick Lube. Phil has contracted with Oscar Smith, a process improvement consultant, to help him better understand operations and improve profitability. Oscar has used the observation method to generate a flowchart of Activity 2, Write Service Order. The resulting flowchart begins with Figure 6.10 and continues with Figure 6.11 and Figure 6.12.

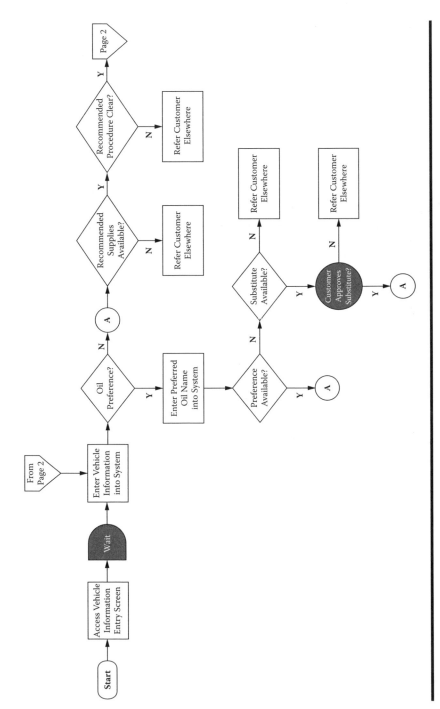

Figure 6.10 Activity view of Phil's Quick Lube oil change (Activity 2–Write Service Order) using a flowchart.

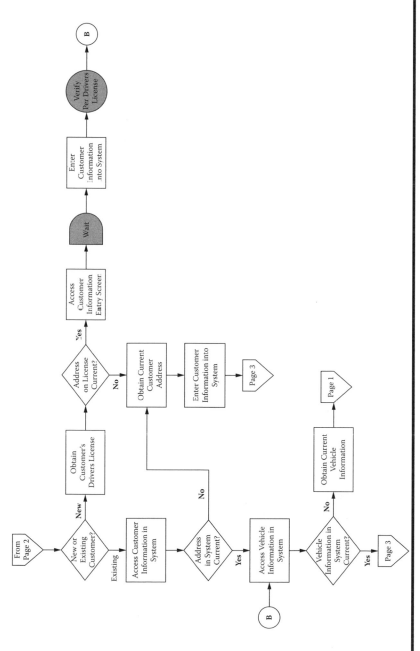

Figure 6.11 (Continued) Activity view of Phil's Quick Lube oil change (Activity 2–Write Service Order) using a flowchart.

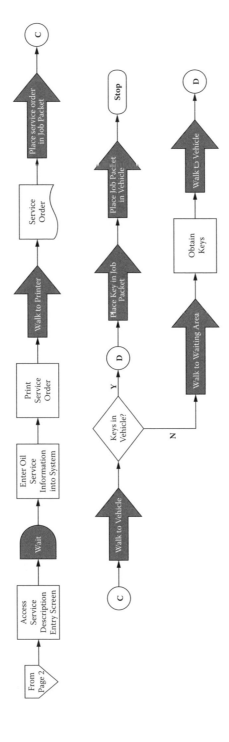

Figure 6.12 (Continued) Activity view of Phil's Quick Lube oil change (Activity 2–Write Service Order) using a flowchart.

Interpreting Flowcharts

A flowchart is a graphic representation of the sequence of work that makes up an activity. I tend to use flowcharts to understand work at the most granular level. If you use them the way I suggest in this chapter, it will help you identify waste or nonvalue-creating work and perhaps document that waste for others to see. You may not want to take the time to select and use the right symbols to show the waste once you have discovered it if you have already decided to eliminate that work. Stated another way, I would use the symbols to help analyze the way the work is done currently. After improving the work, if you draw a flowchart for that work, it will use very different symbols.

At any rate, the more intelligence built into the flowchart, the greater its usefulness. By intelligence, I mean the use of symbols to represent what actually takes place in the work. Most users of flowcharts tend to rely on very few symbols and, thus, limit the tools usefulness. (It's not the number or variety of symbols per se that makes the flow chart useful, it's whether you are using enough symbols to help you recognize where waste, delays, rework, etc. occur in a process).

A flowchart helps you quickly identify how complicated an activity really is and where waste in the work occurs.

Interpreting the Flowchart for Activity 2

How might you interpret the flowchart and information you have gained thus far? Consider the following questions as you refer to Figure 6.10 through Figure 6.12.

1. What are the boundaries of the work shown in this map?
   a. Activity 2, Write Service Order: The work starts at the point where vehicle information obtained from the customer is entered into the Vehicle Information entry screen. The work ends by placing a job packet containing the written service order and vehicle key in the driver's vehicle.
2. What components of work does this map show?
   a. Activities: an input and an output
   b. Resources: computer and printer (these are called out as part of the activities)

   What features of work does it show?
   a. Value-creating and nonvalue-creating activities

4. What properties of work does it show?
   a. Value, Waste (resource utilization)
5. Are you able to trace the flow of the major input as it is converted into an output?
   a. Yes, the major **input** of customer *information* gets entered into a computer and ends up in a **written service order**. Two other inputs are an *empty* job packet and the vehicle keys. The service order and keys are placed in the *empty* job packet; the *full* job packet is placed in the vehicle.
6. Is there any waste present?
   a. Yes, mostly motion, and some inspection. There are lots of decisions in the current work. If the customer is new, they may all be necessary. If it is an existing customer, you may be able to skip this activity entirely.

Chapter 7

Seven Principles to Improve Flow

Overview

In this chapter, I introduce a set of 7 principles and 29 associated guidelines that will help you improve "flow" in knowledge work. I'll use information from an actual client engagement that illustrates how these principles may be applied in a knowledge work setting. To preserve anonymity, all I'll say is that the client was a large Dod organization whose name rhymes with "wavy."

I'll show you the results of the engagement, and then I'll "walk you through" each of the principles and guidelines so that you may better understand how they were applied. Of the three map types this book covers, the Cross-functional Process Map (Swimlane Diagram) was used exclusively during this engagement.

Throughout his chapter, I use the "working definitions" provided in Chapter 2 for the following concepts:

- Work Boundaries, Components, Features, Properties
- Workflow
- Flow

The three main sections of this chapter are organized as follows:

I. Background of the Engagement
  • Purpose

- Improvement Goal
- Improvement Team's Summary Results
  - o Figure 7.1 Summary Results
- How Work is Organized
  - o Headquarters
  - o Field
  - o Improvement Project Team
  - o What is a "Funding Document?"
  - o Commercial Equivalent of this Work

II. The Significance of a "Serial" Workflow and "Handoffs"
- Key Features of a Serial Workflow
  - o Figure 7.2 Features of Serial Workflows
- Features of the Funding Document Workflow
- Components and Features of Knowledge Work "Handoffs"
  - o Information inputs
  - o IT Systems and Databases
  - o The Knowledge Worker
- What is "Flow?"
  - o Figure 7.3 What is "Flow?"

III. Seven Principles to Improve the Flow of Knowledge Work
1. Improve Flow from the Outside-in
   a. Five Guidelines
   b. What the team learned
2. Measure what Matters to the Customer
   a. Five Guidelines
   b. What the team learned
      i. Table 7.1 Selected measures of flow
      ii. Table 7.2 Initial measurement data established by the team
3. Make the end-to-end Flow Visible
   a. Five Guidelines
   b. What the team learned
4. Identify and Remove Barriers to Flow
   a. Four Guidelines
      i. Table 7.3 Types of Waste in Knowledge-Intensive Work
      ii. Table 7.4 Components with Features that Help or Hinder Flow
      iii. Table 7.5 List and Definition of "Enabler's" Used to Assess the Workflow
   b. What the team learned
      i. Problematic Components and Features of Knowledge Work
      1. Workflow Design

      2. Information Systems

      3. Motivation and Measurement

      4. Human Resources

      5. Policies and Rules

      6. Facilities

5. Connect and align value added work fragments

    a. Four Guidelines

    b. What the team learned

6. Organize around the end to end flow

    a. Two Guidelines

    b. What the team learned

7. Manage the flow visually

    a. Three Guidelines

    b. What the team learned

There are many lessons learned, suggestions, and observations contained in the engagement "narrative." Most if not all of these are applicable to *any* knowledge work or business process – you won't need to enlist in one of the armed forces to gain the benefits.

As you read this chapter, be on the lookout for:

1. A key feature of knowledge work is that the workflow often exhibits a serial pattern.
2. Within a workflow with a serial pattern, there are specific forms of waste and barriers to flow that frequently occur and are hiding in plain sight.
3. Barriers to flow cause work to take longer, cost more, and produce less.
4. Use some type of systematic approach to assess a workflow (to identify causes of waste and surface barriers to flow).
5. Measures of flow and waste should be used to quantify workflow performance.
6. Value creating time (VCT), Lead-time (LT), VCT/LT, and percent Complete and Accurate are especially useful measures.
7. The seven principles and associated guidelines will help you *dramatically* shorten lead-time, reduce cost, and increase productivity in any type of knowledge work or business process, i.e., for both profit, and nonprofit corporations, including financial services, hospitals, and government (all three levels).

I. Background of the Engagement

Purpose of the Engagement

1. Use Lean-thinking principles to improve a knowledge work process.
2. Build skills so that the improvement team members would be able to apply what they learn *immediately.*
3. Demonstrate "proof of concept." This was the first attempt to use Lean thinking at Headquarters, so leadership had a keen interest in the results.

The process selected for improvement was called the "funding document process." See "What is a Funding Document?" immediately after the discussion of "How Work is Organized."

Improvement Goal (for the "Funding Document Process")

Reduce "funding document" lead-time (ideally to two days or less).

Note: To put this goal in context, at the outset we did not know the lead-time "baseline" number. It turned out to be 28 days on average. Talk about a *stretch* goal!

Improvement Team's Summary Results

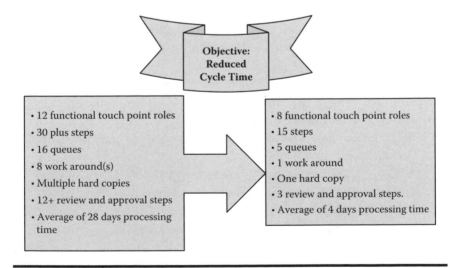

Figure 7.1   Summary results.

How Work Is Organized

There are two organizations involved: Headquarters (HQ) and Field.

At Headquarters, work is organized into Program Executive Offices (PEO), and functional competencies, such as Finance, Contracts, Engineering, Comptroller, and Accounting.

The work done by a PEO is associated with one or more individual programs. Program managers organize the work by project teams.

The functional competencies do work that supports the work of the programs and projects. The individuals who do this work often support several programs and many projects.

Project teams and functional competencies also accomplish the work done in the field.

The funding document process that the improvement team examined focused on project level work and involved both project leader and functional competency roles (such as comptroller), both at HQ and the Field.

Here is an overview of what happens:

Work Done at Headquarters

1. Project leader creates a plan, budget, and schedule to perform work.
2. Budget estimates from all projects are compiled and become an input (part of the overall DoD budget request) to the U.S. Congress.
3. Congress appropriates money for the DoD, i.e., the annual defense budget is passed and signed by the president.
4. The amount appropriated may be less, more, or the same as the funds requested.
5. The appropriated amount (lump sum) is sent to HQ, which allocates portions to each Program Executive Office and, subsequently, to individual projects.
6. Project leaders now know what their budgets are.
7. Before money may be spent, and the work to be done by the field may begin, several criteria must be met:
   a. Funds (money) must be traceable to line items in the approved Congressional Appropriation.
   b. There are eight different categories of funds, i.e., "colors of money." Each category may be used for a specific type of work only. There are three conditions related to the purpose, timing, and amount of funds that must be met to spend the funds. For example, you can't use funds designated for facilities to pay salaries; you must use the funds during the same fiscal year for which it is budgeted, and you can't "spend

more" than the budgeted amount, even if the work is not completed. In practice these three conditions are verified by the HQ Comptroller, since by regulation, only the Comptroller role may "accept" or "transfer" funds. Each project leader must link the right funds to the right work, and then be able to track and monitor the work to be performed and the use of funds against the project plan, budget, and schedule.

c. Each project leader must link the *right* funds to the *right* work, and then be able to track and monitor the work to be performed and the use of funds against the project plan, budget, and schedule.

Work Done in the Field

d. Money received from HQ also must match the planned purpose, amount, and timeframe. This is the same as 7b above, but now these conditions are to be verified by the Field comptroller.

e. Must be ready and able to perform the planned work in the same timeframe per the HQ project plan, budget, and schedule.

f. Must be able to track and report funds use and work progress/results within its field planning, budgeting mechanisms, and also to the HQ project.

Improvement Project Team (Team)

The team (18 people in total) consisted of two "natural" workgroups, comprised of HQ and Field personnel, plus two senior leaders from the HQ Comptroller and HQ Financial Management organizations, respectively. Each natural workgroup was largely composed of Finance, Accounting, Budgeting, and Comptroller personnel.

What Is a Funding Document?

The **funding document** is the mechanism used to create and document the linkages and verifications (above list: 7a–f); it is also used to transfer or receive funds (from one comptroller to another). The annual volume of funding document transactions (for all HQ-initiated work) is in the thousands. The dollar volume was approximately $8 billion.

Commercial Equivalent

The commercial business equivalent to the above would involve annual operating budgets, a project portfolio, and project managers who contract (via a statement of work, sales order, work order, or purchase order (PO)) with another part of the business (or use outside services) to perform some portion of the project deliverables.

The project managers would track and monitor the work and cost in accordance with the project plan, schedule, and budget. The entity (supplier or vendor) doing the work would provide periodic work progress reports and use invoices or some other mechanism to bill for the work. The linkage to be made is between the invoice, PO, and project plan, budget, and statement of work.

II. The Significance of a "Serial" Workflow and "Handoffs"

Key Features of a Serial Workflow

Figure 7.2 depicts a serial workflow and highlights several associated features, including handoffs. Refer to Chapter 5 to see these and other types of workflow patterns such as collaborative and parallel.

Serial workflows are prevalent in knowledge work.

Features of the Funding Document Workflow

Here are some features of the "Funding Document" workflow.

1. The workflow exhibits a "serial" pattern, i.e. one activity after another in a linear sequence. This is often the case when the original input was a paper form that was routed for inputs, reviews, or approval. Note that I've included a generic example of a serial workflow for illustration purposes, rather than the actual map the team created.
2. The workflow *starts* when a "trigger" of some type occurs. It *ends* with a *countable result* or *item* that exits the workflow and becomes an input to a "downstream" or external customer.
3. The workflow involves two distinct organizations (HQ and Field) and several functions, disciplines, and roles within each. (12 distinct roles were involved).
4. Throughout the workflow, there are many (at least 12) *handoffs* that involve many different roles. See discussion of "handoffs" below.
5. There are many (12+) reviews or approvals that take place throughout the workflow.

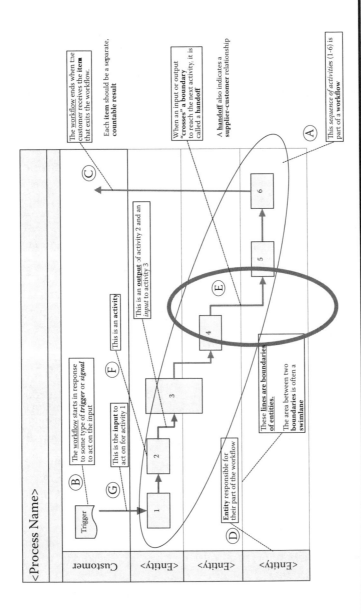

Figure 7.2   Serial workflow pattern in swimlane diagram.

6. The main results or items from the workflow are a "go/no go" decision(s), and action(s) to notify customers and other stakeholders directly affected. "Go/no go" means a set of readiness criteria to be met in order to proceed. (7a–f, under "How Work is Organized").

7. A set of information inputs associated with each criterion is required to make the decision; completeness and accuracy of the information inputs is a key consideration. Additionally there are legal and regulatory requirements associated with one of the criteria that must be met.

8. The information inputs come from different roles, functions, disciplines, and IT systems.

9. Some portions of the decision may only be made by a specific role (Comptroller) according to current regulations.

10. This workflow is pervasive; it is a "routine transaction" that is performed many times by every project; there may be hundreds of projects underway throughout the Enterprise.

These 10 features describe the funding document workflow. Over time, I've learned that these same features are also typical of most knowledge-intensive workflows, and the serial pattern occurs with much greater frequency than other workflow patterns such as collaborative, or parallel.

Serial workflows *always* have handoffs. (There were 12 in the funding document workflow).

When you find a handoff, you should take a closer look at it.

Components and Features of Knowledge Work Handoffs

What happens at a handoff?

Lots. Every handoff is a supplier-customer relationship, usually between different roles.

Knowledge work handoffs typically involve these three work components as a minimum:

■ Information and know-how (resource) inputs
■ IT systems
■ The person who performs each role

Each of these components exhibits problematic features usually present in every knowledge work or business process handoff. Why problematic? They act as "barriers to flow." I'll have more to say on barriers to flow when I "walk you through" principle 4.

Information Inputs

1. In knowledge work, the main resource inputs are often information and expertise (know-how.) *This contrasts with manufacturing work, which often features raw material, parts, or subassemblies as the main input.*
2. The work that each input represents varies, and often varies widely. Inputs may arrive one at a time or in batches. The inputs aren't labeled in a way that would help distinguish one type of work activity from any other, or, the amount of work each input represents. (They all show up as incoming emails; usually the email is communicating information *about the input* rather than serving as the input).
3. Like most knowledge workers, there are always many emails in the inbox. So, every time a handoff occurs, (a new email arrives) a delay occurs as well. Only one item can be worked on at a time, so the other items wait. Items also wait for the person to open and read each email in order to know what type of work it represents. This is the equivalent to work in process inventory in a manufacturing plant.
4. Delays also occur when there is no easily recognized "trigger" which signals the performer to act on an input for a **specific** item and work-flow. Emails and the work each represents are "undifferentiated;" they all come to a single inbox though each represents work that is unique to and a part of one distinct workflow. Think, "one size fits all."

Information Technology (IT) Systems

1. IT systems are frequently the main "tools" used by knowledge workers.
2. Access to the available information, and the IT systems that contain that information, is often based on the role and functional department of the performer.
3. No single role has access to the complete set of inputs needed to support the decision to be made.
4. Likewise, no single IT system contains the complete set of inputs required to support the decision.

The Knowledge Worker

1. The knowledge worker who performs an activity generally has many other additional work responsibilities (*each often associated with a unique work-flow*). A given work activity may not be that persons main responsibility, so only a portion of their time is available for this activity. This seems to make sense, *until the realization occurs that the activity is part of a cross-functional workflow that has its own timing requirements.* The timing of both rarely is "in-sync" without some form of explicit coordination and scheduling among the affected parties.

2. Knowledge workers are often *physically dispersed*; they are located on different floors, different buildings, different cities, time zones, etc. The same is true for the organizations each represents. *No line of sight exists; the location or identity of the other members of the natural workgroup is often unknown.*

3. Each knowledge worker does his or her work in a "cube-farm." Within the cube-farm, "clusters" of people organized by role and functional department may sit together. For instance, a group of budget analysts may sit together in an area designated for accounting personnel. *Typically, neither item flow nor workflow(s) are visible in this arrangement.*

4. When a knowledge worker receives an email (see 2–4 under "Information Inputs") they have no way of linking that email to the appropriate work flow *without opening and reading each one individually.*

I believe the work features I've described thus far are highly representative of knowledge-work in general. If you encounter or experience these in your workplace, you are certainly not alone.

But there is hope.

I've devoted the rest of the chapter to a set of principles and guidelines that will help you improve "flow" (see Figure 7.3) in knowledge work or a business process. I've developed and made use of these over many years.

They work.

I'll describe how the team applied each of the seven principles and what they learned when they did so. I'll also walk you through the guidelines associated with each principle.

What Is "Flow?"

Figure 7.3 illustrates several characteristics of "Flow."

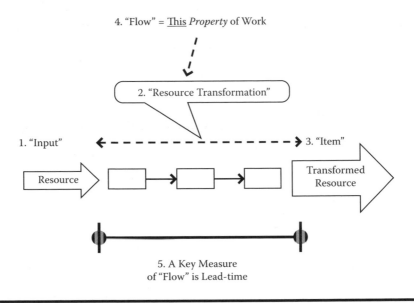

Figure 7.3   What is flow?

1. A *resource* "input" gets transformed into another customer-valued form.
2. The *resource transformation* takes place via one or more *value-creating* activities.
3. The *resource* has been transformed; it is now an "item." Synonyms for "item" are output, product, or service.
4. Flow is the *property* of work that corresponds to the *resource transformation*.
5. Lead-time (elapsed time from input to item) is a key measure of flow.

In knowledge work especially, a resource input is generally in one of three *states*:

1. Waiting
2. "Being worked on"
3. "Being moved"

"Flow," corresponds to the "*being worked* on" *state*. Ideally, "flow" consists of 100 percent value-creating work activities. The two remaining *states* (waiting, or being moved) are forms of *waste*.

"Lead-time" includes the elapsed time for all three states. So, when you improve "flow" you eliminate or greatly reduce waste, which also reduces the lead-time. The value-creating time (VCT) is now a greater percentage of lead-time (LT). I cover this further as part of Principle 2: Measure what Matters to the Customer.

III. Seven Principles to Improve the Flow of Knowledge Work

Seven Principles for Improving Flow

1. Improve flow from the outside in
2. Measure what matters to the customer
3. Make the end-to end (flow) visible
4. Identify and remove barriers to flow
5. Connect and align value-added work fragments
6. Organize around the end-to-end flow
7. Manage the flow visually

Principle 1: Improve Flow from the Outside In

Five guidelines to improve flow from the outside in:

1. Identify the item or work product that exits the workflow
2. Make sure the item is specific, and is a countable result
3. Determine who is the customer for that item or work product
4. Find out what the customer values about that item
5. Learn from the customer what the "nature of demand" is for the item

Natural work groups usually want to talk about the *activities* they perform. Though activities are what they know best, the focus should be on *Items*. Start with the work item or work product you provide to the downstream customer who is the recipient of the item and trace its path upstream, or from the outside in. This focuses the improvement on changes to work that customers see or experience, and that *create value*. From the customer's perspective, any other work doesn't really matter.

What the Team Learned from the "Outside In" Principle (1)

Identify the Item or Work Product That Exits the Workflow Principle (2)

The item initially was (thought to be) the funding document. But what matters most is the resultant decision and subsequent actions that the funding document facilitates. If you think only of the funding document as a discrete form, it limits the solution space you consider when re-designing the work in some way.

Make Sure the Item Is Specific and Is a Countable Result

By specific, I mean uniquely identifiable. Often there is a class or category that first comes to mind, such as contracts or financial reports. Items within the second category might be a profit and loss statement, a balance sheet, or an accounts receivable aging analysis, etc.

One of the reasons this is so important is that the workflow that produces each item is distinct. You need to be able to observe the actual flow of the item.

It turns out that "funding documents" is a class. Who knew?

The team focused on one type known as a "reimbursable funding document." It is used with work that is performed by Field activities (another part of the "wavy.") Each reimbursable funding document can be counted.

Determine Who Is the Customer for That Item or Work Product

At the outset, there was confusion about who the customer was. This is quite common in knowledge work, by the way. Virtually everyone thought the customer was the "warfighter." The warfighter is the most downstream, external customer. But, they can't do much damage to the enemy with a *reimbursable funding document.* The warfighter eventually receives a very different item. One better suited to their mission.

For this type of funding document, there were two customers. One was the HQ project leader that initiated the funding request. The item they received was notification that funding was "in place."

The second customer was the downstream (Field) project leader who was being asked to do the work. The item he/she received was notification that funds for this work were available and had been accepted by the Field comptroller. This meant work could start in the field.

Note that for both customers, the team discovered that the item was the *notification.* This generally took the form of an e-mail in the current workflow.

Find Out What the Customer Values about That Item

Because the customers had just now been defined, we had to go talk to them to find out what they valued about this item. No one had asked the project leaders this question before. The answer turned out to be "turnaround time." So then we asked what they thought was a good turnaround time. The answer was a couple of days. This information was translated into "lead time of two days" and became the goal of the first project during the engagement.

Learn from the Customer What the "Nature Of Demand*" Is for the Item

This guideline helps you understand the level of performance the workflow must meet and to determine what the workload will be to do so. Some considerations to help you better understand demand may include:

Volume = How many
Frequency = How often
Timing = When
How predictable is the demand?

I did not ask the team to do this initially as part of the "what do you value" question. However, during the course of the engagement, the team started analyzing historical information and also went back to the project leaders to try to better understand demand. No one had discussed demand with the project leaders before, but once the team asked, the project leaders also wanted to know the answers if and when the team could figure this out.

This conveniently brings us to the next principle.

Principle 2: Measure What Matters to the Customer

Five guidelines to measure what matters to the customer:

1. Use measures related to the flow of the item.
2. Measure the characteristics of flow that relate directly to what the customer values.
3. Whenever possible, incorporate measures into the daily work, i.e., real-time integrated in the workflow.
4. Only collect data that you actually use.

---

* John Seddon, *Freedom from Command and Control*, Productivity Press, 2005, 47.

5. Use flow-centric measurement data as "real-time performance indicators," the way you do the gauges on the dashboard while you are driving.

What the Team Learned from the "Measure What Matters" Principle (2)

Use Measures Related to the Flow of the Item

Often, in knowledge-intensive work, there are few measures in place that relate to flow (see Table 7.1).

Prior to this project, I'm pretty sure that the funding document workflow had not been systematically examined or assessed using any of the measures listed in Table 7.1. So, there was no existing data related to flow that the team and I could use to help us determine our baseline performance. Initially, we had no idea how difficult it may be to achieve a two-day lead time. We didn't know what the lead time was currently. We did not know the capability of the current workflow. Nor did we have existing data on the nature of customer demand, or the extent to which that demand was being met.

You should expect the same situation. The lack of measures and data that relate to "flow" is quite common in knowledge work.

What do you do? You make an estimate, start to collect it, or very often, you do both.

The team was very resourceful. They did both. They learned that, on average, the current lead time was estimated at 28 days. How? They took a sample of actual, recently completed funding documents and reverse-engineered the end-to-end transaction for each of them. Many, but not all, of the steps of the workflow were done using IT systems; some of these systems included time stamp information, for example. E-mails had dates as well.

You use what you have as best you can initially. For example (Table 7.2) the team came up with the following based on observation of the work and review of the process map they created.

Even without data for many measures of flow, the team recognized that *if they could find a way to eliminate queues, review and approval steps, and other types of waste*, the reduction in lead-time would be dramatic.

It may seem counter-intuitive, but once the team began to think through what the measures of flow would tell them (had they existed), they became very energized. They really wanted to find ways to meet the target of two days.

Table 7.1   Selected Measures of Flow

Name of Measure	Related Work Property	Definition
Lead time (LT)	Flow; Resource utilization: Value + waste (cumulative from all activities end-to-end)	Elapsed time for a work item to progress or flow through all the activities that take place between the *two external boundaries,* i.e., of a *defined amount of work,* such as a workflow, process, or value stream
Cycle time (CT)	Flow; Resource utilization: Value + waste (at a single activity)	Elapsed time that a resource is applied during an activity to create the output from that activity
		In knowledge work, this measure is not well understood, and is often confused with lead time
		Here is an example. The elapsed time the computer is used often differs from that of the time spent by the person using the computer to create value. You wait while the computer boots up, opens an application or refreshes a screen, then you begin the value-creating activity
Value-creating time (VCT)	Resource utilization: Value	Elapsed time *used to create value,* i.e., transform a resource in a way that customers value
Complete and Accurate (%C&A)	Quality (of a single supplier–customer hand off, i.e., output crosses interface)	Perception of customer that the information they receive contains everything they require and that the information is also correct
		This is a great measure for monitoring hand-offs between upstream and downstream work done by different people
		(continued)

Table 7.1 Selected Measures of Flow (Continued)

Name of Measure	Related Work Property	Definition
First-pass yield (FPY) or rolled throughput yield (RTY)	Quality (through all the activities within a workflow)	"Yield" (Y) is a measure of percentage defect-free items (outputs) at an individual activity. "First-Pass Yield" is cumulative, i.e., a measure of the percentage defect-free outputs through *all* the activities $Y_1 \times Y_2 \times Y_n = FPY$
Throughput volume/time period	Resource utilization: Productivity	Number of items completed per unit of time (sec, hr, day, month, etc.)

Table 7.2 Initial Measurement Data Established by the Team

Some Baseline Count Data	Some Implications
Twelve roles	At least 12 hand offs (see queues below), many opportunities for errors and rework loops
Thirty-one steps	At least six were 100 percent rework
Sixteen queues	Sixteen sources of delays, each with its own duration (think e-mails in in-boxes)
Twelve + review and approval steps	Ten or so more delays; this type of step is usually nonvalue-creating; 38 percent of the total steps are probably waste
Multiple hard copies	A form of waste, also reduces amount of time available to do value-creating work
Eight work-arounds	Most were symptoms of unmet IT system requirements

Measure the Characteristics of Flow That Relate Directly to What the Customer Values

Recall the customer decided that turnaround time was important. Project leaders defined this as "from the time I initiate the request to the time I receive notification back that the funding is in place."

The team recognized that a good measure for "start to finish turn-around" is lead time. They also learned that "start" began when the customer initiated the request, rather than when they first began working on that request. Likewise, "finish" meant when the customer received the notification, not when they sent it. They also realized that "complete and accurate" would be a critical measure in the future.

I've already mentioned that in the current workflow there were no measures of flow. Consequently, the best opportunity for the team to apply the next three guidelines would be as part of a "future state" workflow design.

Whenever Possible, Incorporate Measures into the Work Itself

By incorporated, I mean "built in" or integrated in the workflow, such that doing the work also generates the measures around that work.

This is often addressed in the *design* of the *workflow* itself, and in knowledge work that usually means designing the IT system so that it provides this data with no additional burden on those doing the work.

Only Collect Data That You Actually Use

The idea is to use the *knowledge* you may gain from a measure-to-maintain or improve flow, not to record and report it to someone else. The "you" in this case refers to those in the natural workgroup who do this work.

Use Flow-Centric Measurement Data as "Real-Time Performance Indicators"

Like the gauges on the dashboard while you are driving, measures of flow are most useful in real time, that is, while the work is flowing. At the risk of oversimplifying, you want your measures to tell you "the flow is operating as it should" or "something is wrong."

Principle 3: Make the End-to-End Flow Visible

I recommend that *each* member of the natural work group apply the following guidelines *individually,* then work together as a team to create one workflow model that reflects what they observed.

Five guidelines to make the end-to-end flow visible.

1. Trace the *actual* path of the item, from the initial trigger to the point in the workflow where the customer receives the item.
2. Identify the main resources involved along the path.
3. Observe an *item* as it flows along the path; watch while the work is being done
4. Select or define a method to literally make the (item) flow visible in the context of the workflow in which it occurs.
5. Determine how this workflow relates to the organization's primary workflow (order to delivery).

What the Team Learned from the "Make the Flow Visible" Principle (3)

Trace the *Actual* Path of the Item, from the Initial Trigger to the Point in the Workflow Where the Customer Receives the Item

Don't forget, work from the *outside in* when you do this.

One of the distinguishing features of "flow" in knowledge work is that it's *not visible, i.e.* much of the work takes place in people's heads, in their computers, or most often a combination of both. Knowledge workers frequently don't know what occurs before, or after their "part" of each workflow, or what activities the computer is actually performing. ("Enter data into the xx screen) does not describe what *happens* to that data.

So, the intent of this guideline is to:

■ establish the starting and ending boundaries of the end to end workflow
■ determine the initial (and subsequent) "trigger(s)," or what is it that starts action on the input
■ identify the series, sequence, and boundaries of the activities that comprise the workflow (done by people and by IT systems)
■ determine the actual path that connects the activities and along which the item "flows"

These actions help establish the **workflow** *context.*

The reason I suggest that you have each member of the natural workgroup do this is so that each person throughout the workflow may better understand the "part/whole" context for the work he/she does, and especially what happens immediately before and after "his/her" activity. This makes the supplier–customer relationships visible and much stronger to each person.

The team was made up of members that were two distinct natural workgroups. Each workgroup performed the "same" workflow, so once they made the flow visible for their own workflow, they also had the chance to compare one another's as well. They learned they had some of the same activities, some activities differed, and that many activities had the same name (review and approval) but had different meanings and used different methods.

Identify the Main Resources Involved along the Path

The "path" involves *a set of resources* that are transformed, acted upon, and applied during each of the activities. The highlight of this guideline is to "inventory" the set of resources required to do the work. In discussing the next principle, I will explain other considerations associated with resources.

The team used a worksheet I created to help them gather and structure this information, so they could compare and discuss what they found.

Observe an Item as It Flows along the Path; Watch While the Work Is Being Done

Keep in mind that you really aren't trying to document how-to level detail; you're trying to *characterize* or *describe a day in the life of the resources used* throughout the workflow. For example, as you watch a particular activity where data are accessed from an IT system, you learn that to get to the two data elements needed, you must go through nine different screens, each screen takes about 30 seconds to refresh, and that you have to go through the first eight to get to the ninth, which is where the two data elements appear.

There is no need at this point to try and understand what is on any of the nine screens, or what takes place within an activity.

What happens if you are unable to do this (observe the work) in real-time? Time to improvise.

One alternative is to ask them to show you what happens, that is, to demonstrate the activity for you on an actual item as if they were teaching someone new to this task. A second alternative is to ask for a walk-through of the activity without actually doing it. The least useful approach would be to interview someone away from the location where they do the work. It's better than nothing, but you don't get a chance to see them interact with the other resources they use, such as the IT systems, and other equipment, such as printers or faxes. So you usually end up observing this work later, so you understand the significance of what was said and what wasn't in the interview.

When the team did their observations, they discovered the queues and where each occurred. They also found and described "workarounds," steps where multiple hard copies were made, along with why hard copies were being made. They made notes about the physical layout of equipment, file cabinets, printers, and fax machines, cube location, and work signage as well. They noted what they saw on the structured worksheet.

Select or Define a Method to Make the Flow and the Main Resources Involved Visible in the Context of the Workflow Architecture

When you do this for the "as is" or "current state" of the workflow, you most often create some type of explicit workflow model, such as a swimlane diagram or value-stream map. When you do this for the "to be" or "future state," you may end up physically rearranging the workflow and resources so that the path is shorter and more direct, all required resources (and only those required) are available, and the people doing the work have a clear line of sight to each other and of the flow of the item, in real time.

The team created a cross-functional process map (swimlane diagram) to depict the flow and to illustrate the locations where the flow slowed down, stopped, waited, was moved, and where it "looped back" to an earlier activity.

Note: One of the challenges here will be avoiding unnecessary detail *on the process m*ap. At this point, you want to focus on *depicting flow and resources,* not what goes on during each activity.

Determine How This Workflow Relates to the Organization's Primary Workflow (Order to Delivery)

It turns out that this workflow is part of the HQ primary workflow.

Let's recap. So far I've described some key features of serial workflows and what goes on during a handoff. Then I covered three principles and their associated guidelines, along with examples of how the team applied each and what they learned when they did so.

Principle 1 (outside in) helps you identify the boundaries of a specific workflow, the item it produces, the customer who receives the item, what the customer values about the item they receive, and what the nature of customer demand is for that item.

Principle 2 (measure what matters) provides a set of measures that you can use to measure *characteristics of flow that matter to the customer.*

Principle 3 (make flow visible) uses some type of workflow model to make the architecture and the main components visible, depicts the item flow, and what happens along the path the item follows throughout the workflow.

Up to this point, we've focused on and established the boundaries of the workflow.

Now the focus shifts to the (resource) components, individually and collectively. It is time to assess how the relevant resources are deployed, how they currently operate, how connected they are with each other, and what impact they have on "flow." I use the acronym DOC (deployment, operation and connections) for shorthand.

We assess the workflow when we apply the next principle.

Principle 4: Identify and Remove Barriers to Flow

Four guidelines to identify and remove barriers to flow.

1. Identify the types of waste and any "barriers to flow" present
2. Locate the points in the workflow where these occur
3. Determine causes of the waste and why the barrier to flow exists
4. Develop and implement an integrated set of countermeasures that address the causes and remove the barriers

To get the most from applying the guidelines, there are three key concepts to understand:

■ Waste
■ Barrier to flow
■ Countermeasure

What Is Waste?

Any activity that consumes resources, but does not create or add value is considered waste.

Table 7.3 defines and gives examples for each of the types of waste that typically occur in knowledge-intensive work.

Table 7.3   Types of Waste in Knowledge-Intensive Work

Type of Waste	Definition	Knowledge-Intensive Work Example
Overproducing	More or sooner than is really needed right now by the customer	Purchasing or creating anything before it is needed
Inventory	Any form of batch processing, or work-in-process	Work held in in-boxes, storage of office supplies, partially completed tasks or documents, files, online or electronic storage
Waiting	Delays	Time spent pending review or approval; time watching logon, screen refresh, or retrieval or manipulation of information
Extra Processing	Time spent doing unnecessary steps	Rekeying or reformatting data; extra copies or unneeded reports, multiple drafts or versions of presentations, briefings, budgets, plans, etc.
Correction	Any form of defects or rework	Missing (incomplete) or incorrect data or information
Excess Motion	Movement of people	Retrieving anything essential to the task at hand that is "out of reach," such as data, information, files, centralized in-boxes, bookshelves, office supplies, instructions, printers, fax or copy machines
Transportation	Movement of work between locations, offices, floors, buildings, systems, and people	E-mail attachments, documents or files routed for multiple approvals or reviews; expertise or information needed is dispersed rather than co-located or aggregated

What Is a Barrier to Flow?

I use the term *barrier to flow* to refer to any work component (activities, artifacts, resources) with features or which interacts with other components *under current conditions* to hinder flow. Current conditions would include: how the resources are deployed, how they operate currently, and how effective the connections are

Table 7.4   Components with Features that Help or Hinder Flow

This Component ...	With These Features, Helps Flow	With These Features, Hinders Flow
Activity	It's value-creating	It's not value-creating, i.e., waste
Workflow Design	Visible item flow	Item flow not visible
Path	Short, unidirectional "path"	Long, multidirectional "path" with "loopbacks"
Series of Activities	No handoffs, collaborative pattern	Many handoffs, serial pattern
Resources (Required)	All required resources are available when needed	*Any* required resource is not available when needed
People (interdependent natural workgroup)	Co-located	Dispersed in multiple locations
Equipment, or files	Located in easy reach	Located down the hall

between interdependent resources or components with respect to the flow of an item. (Resource deployment, operation, and connections are shortened to DOC.)

Remember, *items* flow. Interactions among components create the item. Each item has its own workflow, and the path the item follows links and involves a distinct set of resources (components) throughout *that* workflow.

Barriers to flow are not absolute categorizations, they are situational. So, the same component with one set of features may help flow, but with different features (the same component) may hinder flow (see Table 7.4).

The approach I used to help the team *identify* barriers to flow was to "assess the workflow by *enabler*" (see Table 7.5). This approach is a subset of what Alec Sharp refers to as a "structured assessment," in the second edition of *Workflow Modeling* (Artech House, 2009), by Alec Sharp and Patrick McDermott. Sharp defines an enabler as a "factor that can be adjusted to impact process performance."

I used a "learn–do" approach with the full team so that they could conduct the assessment. (Recall that one of the purposes of the engagement was skill building and immediate application; another was to demonstrate "proof of

Table 7.5   List and Definition of Enabler's Used to Assess the Workflow

Enabler	Definition	Examples
Workflow Design	How the work, "*works*"; design architecture of the relevant activities and components used to transform a specific *input* into a unique *item*	Anything that "holds the work" people, organization, information system, machinery, in-box, etc.
Information Systems	Information Technology (IT)	Systems, information, computers, voice and data networks, etc.
Motivation and Measurement	How people, organizations, and processes are measured and assessed, and the associated consequences	Explicit and implicit reward systems, incentives. Quantitative level of a work property.
Human Resources	People development and deployment	Work or job design, cross-training, physical or virtual arrangement of structural components such as teams, projects, departments, etc.
Policies and Rules	Operating principles, guidelines established by the enterprise to guide or constrain business processes; laws and regulations	"Invoices will be paid monthly, in the order received"; "the corporate income tax rate is 35 percent"
Facilities	Workplace design and physical infrastructure	Physical layout of such relevant components as equipment, furnishings, machinery; ambient lighting, air quality, noise, energy, natural resources (water, rare earth minerals)

concept" of Lean thinking, and most importantly, the third was to improve the funding document process).

Learn-do consisted of reading assignments, short lectures to emphasize key points, and facilitated discussions on all six enablers. I used material from several sections of the first edition of Alec's book as the starting point for much of the learning content. I added "Lean thinking" practices to most of the enablers; I especially added "Lean thinking" measures of flow to the "motivation and measurement" enabler.

Then, I split the team into subgroups, one for each enabler. Each subgroup assessed the workflow for their assigned enabler, documented their findings, and posted those findings on the conference room walls so that the full team could easily read the results from all the subgroups. To assist each subgroup, I created worksheets for each enabler to help structure the assessment and data collection, and to emphasize features of work components I felt were relevant based on my own observations. I provided real-time coaching for their assigned enabler as questions and findings emerged.

None of the enablers are inherently wasteful. Rather, each enabler will manifest itself in some way that is specific to the flow of the item throughout the end-to-end workflow. Your challenge is to *assess each with respect to the impact it has on flow.* In general, features of work may help or hinder flow. Think of components as "variables" that interact collectively to cause flow. You are seeking to understand the impact each of the variables has on flow, both individually and collectively.

What the Team Learned from the "Remove Barriers to Flow" Principle (4)

Identify the *types of waste* or other barriers to flow present in the workflow.

Waste Types Found by the Team

Right after the team learned the seven types of waste, I asked them: "How many types of waste can you find in the current workflow?" They paused, some then began counting out loud. Several then quickly said, "All seven of them."

I'm so proud.

How many are present in your favorite workflow or process?

In particular, the team identified the delays, waiting, and extra processing associated with multiple review and approval steps, along with the queues that occurred at every handoff, as the main contributors to the 28-day lead time. Additionally, they recognized that their respective workplace design and physical cubicle locations led to excess motion, and movement of work, which also contributed to lead time, albeit to a lesser extent. Because the due dates and complexity of each funding document varied, they felt it was likely that some overproducing occurred as well. Finally, they identified "loopbacks" where rework occurred.

Okay, all seven types of waste were present. That may or may not be a big deal. If waste contributes to lead time and there is a lot of waste present, it *is* a big deal.

How can we make this determination?

It turns out that the Boston Consulting Group (BCG) has determined a rule we could use to estimate the amount of waste present.

"The 0.05 to 5 Rule"

In 1990, BCG determined the following:

> Across a spectrum of businesses, the amount of time required to execute a service or an order, manufacture, and deliver a product is far less than the actual time the service or product spends in the value-delivery system.
>
> The 0.05 to 5 rule highlights the poor "time productivity" of most organizations since most products and many services are actually receiving value for only 0.05 to 5 percent of the time they are in the value-delivery systems of their companies.*

If up to 99.95 percent of time spent is waste, this represents a significant opportunity for improvement. Learning to see the waste that is hidden in plain sight is a valuable skill.

This rule tells us we should expect to find a high percentage of waste. However, this is only a rule of thumb, right?

The 0.05 to 5 Rule Applied to the Funding Document Process

Those of you more fluent in "Lean-speak" may be more familiar with the terms *value-creating time* and *lead time*. The 0.05 to 5 rule is the amount of value-creating time expressed as a percentage of total lead time.

How does waste contribute to lead time? It *increases* it.

Lead Time (LT) = Value-Creating Time (VCT) + Non VCT (waste)

I did not ask the team to make this calculation during the engagement.

Here is a quick "back of the envelope" calculation to determine what portion of the 28-day lead time may be waste.

---

* G. Stalk, Jr. and T. Hout. 1990. *Competing against time.* Florence, MA: The Free Press, p. 76.

During one of the pilots of the value-creating activities only, the lowest time was 20 minutes.

Let's assume all 20 minutes consisted of value-creating time.

Lead-time (LT) - Value-Creating Time (VCT) = Non Value-Creating Time (waste)

$$13,440 \text{ min} - 20 \text{ min} = 13,420 \text{ min of non-VCT (waste)}$$

Expressed as a percentage, VCT = .15% of LT (up to 99.85% of time spent in the current workflow may be waste).

$$\text{VCT} = 20 \text{ minutes}$$
$$\text{LT} = 13,440 \text{ minutes (28 days} \times 480 \text{ minutes per day)}$$
$$\text{VCT/LT}$$
$$20 \text{ minutes}/13,440 \text{ minutes} = \textbf{.15\%}$$

Those BCG guys may be on to something.

Barriers to Flow the Team Identified

Identify the types of waste or other *barriers to flow* present in the workflow. I think of the six enablers shown in Table 7.5 as categories of work components. This set of component categories is where you will find many of the usual "barrier to flow" suspects. For each enabler (component), I have listed features that cause waste or hinder flow that I have found occur frequently. I will also discuss some of the 95 findings that the subgroups identified during their assessment.

Problematic Components and Features of Knowledge Work

Problematic Features of Workflow Design

What is it about the current workflow design that causes waste or acts as a barrier to flow? For example, is the flow continuous or is there something in the design of the workflow that causes the flow of an item to slow down or stop, or for items to accumulate?

In my experience, most end-to-end workflows have not been consciously designed for all the required resources to operate as a single coherent whole. One of the reasons for this is that we tend to think of "work" *as part of a job rather than a portion of a workflow.*

Work viewed in this manner leads us to link or associate tasks to jobs *rather than workflows and items*. It also treats resources as costs to be reduced rather than components to be deployed, operated, and connected in such a way as to match item flow to customer demand.

Some features of workflow design that act as barriers to flow include:

1. There are many handoffs, aka touch points or touches (in general, each new handoff involves a new "in-basket" where items wait until acted upon).
2. The path the item follows is complex.
3. The path the item follows is not visible, so no one knows or can see what the status or progress of a specific item is at a glance.
4. One or more required resources is not available when needed.
5. The timing of upstream and downstream activities are out of sync with one another (one way the handoffs mentioned above slow down or stop flow).

Team's Selected Findings Due to Workflow Design

"One Size Fits All"

This enabler had many findings. In addition to the five features shown above, the team recognized the current workflow as a "one size fits all" process. What that means is that every category of funding document (recall that they were focusing on one of four types in this engagement) and items ranging from the very simple to the very complex all went through the same workflow.

Serial Workflow: Too Many Roles Involved

The major decision to be made involved a set of serial, discrete tasks that were dispersed and distributed among many roles. Furthermore, the decision was made at the end of the sequence currently. This sequence and the roles that were allowed to access the data involved were "hard-wired" into the existing IT system. The team determined that most of the value-creating tasks were independent of each other and that the needed data were available much earlier in the sequence.

Problematic Features of Information Systems

Some features of information systems that act as barriers to flow include:

1. Some of the data needed lies outside IT systems.

2. Some of the data needed resides in several IT systems, none of which can "share" that data.
3. Data exists, but not in the form needed (you must compile the "pieces" and then manipulate the "whole" in some way).
4. The same data often has to be re-entered, especially across different functional departments (sales, order entry, accounting, purchasing).
5. Some types of data are only available periodically; you need it before the next period occurs.
6. It takes multiple screens to get to the data you really need.
7. Access to data is determined by role.

Team's Selected Findings Due to Information Systems

The team found this enabler to also be a major source of findings. More importantly, they learned that any potential change to IT would be added to the current backlog of six months. Most of the findings in the list below are variations of those seven features I listed above.

- "Awkward" user interfaces (screens and fields do not relate explicitly to the decision to be made).
- Available information often was in a form that did not speed throughput.
- Portions of the information that was available electronically were located in many different places.
- 100 percent of the information that was needed was not always available (in or out of systems).
- Timing was out of sync with downstream actions.

Problematic Features of Motivation and Measurement

Some features of motivation and measurement that act as barriers to flow include:

1. Existing measures tell you nothing about item flow.
2. Existing measures drive the wrong behavior(s).
3. Rewards are tied to measures that do not relate to flow.
4. Measures relate to features of work that are not under the control of the people whose work is being measured.

Team's Selected Findings Due to Motivation and Measurement

The team felt that "motivation" was part of the human resources enabler. At any rate they didn't have any findings. The team identified the absence of measures related to flow as their finding.

Problematic Features of Human Resources

Some features of human resources that act as barriers to flow include:

1. Priorities, schedule, goals, and measures are set "locally" and, thus, they are not aligned or synchronized throughout the workflow.
2. Criteria for what constitutes excellent quality at the source or "complete and accurate" are missing or ambiguous.

Team's Selected Findings Due to Human Resources

This enabler was another main source of findings. I've previously commented on the first bulleted item shown below. This is a very common characteristic of the approach to staffing knowledge work.

- Shared versus dedicated resources (people split their time among several workflows).
- Priorities set individually (by each role, not item due date for example).
- Priorities across roles and throughout the workflow are out of alignment.
- Decision requirements and criteria for excellence were not explicit; they also were ambiguous.
- Decision requirements spread across many roles.
- Little feedback or guidance was provided (to any role); same errors would occur.

With respect to priorities, the team recognized that each person in the workflow had their own way of deciding in what priority they worked on a given item, and that the priorities were not coordinated or synchronized across the set of roles. (I used the term *locally* to describe this situation in the first barrier to flow above.) This approach will always result in delays, and it is due in large part to the way the jobs were originally designed. It is such common practice among knowledge workers that it is accepted as simply "the way we do our work."

When the team discussed what the phrase *review and approve* meant in actual practice, they realized that no one had a list of the criteria they were using currently or should use, yet this activity took place at least 12 times. Among other things, this meant that no one past the first review and approval step could tell whether an item had previously been reviewed and approved; thus, each role felt as if they were the last line of defense in guarding taxpayer money and did it again *just to be sure*. People learned to do the review and approve activity informally from whoever did it before them; there was no training to do this. There were no examples of items that met the criteria, or didn't meet the criteria, with explanations of why.

The team also noted that no feedback was provided or available to help prevent recurring errors.

Problematic Features of Policies and Rules

Some features of policies and rules that act as barriers to flow include:

1. What "everybody knows" is not written down anyplace, so if the activity is done infrequently or "the person who does this is on vacation," someone new to the job must discover how to do this work all over again.
2. There are strongly or widely held beliefs and assumptions treated as rules, when, in fact, no such "rule" exists.
3. A rule exists ("it's always been that way as long as I can remember"), but, conditions now make the rule unnecessary or even counterproductive.
4. Rules exist (and so do the workarounds and exceptions to the rule).
5. Regulatory or legal requirements become work restrictions that specify a given task may only be done by an explicitly designated role, specialty, or functional discipline.

Team's Selected Findings Due to Policies and Rules

The team verified that there was a regulation that specified, "only the comptroller role may accept or transfer funds."

Problematic Features of Facilities

Some features of facilities that act as barriers to flow include:

1. Resources are dispersed, separated, or unconnected from one another (people who need to collaborate; IT systems that should share data).
2. Required resources are not located at the point of use.
3. There is no line of sight (the physical layout obstructs or hides the path, or the view of the item's progress along that path, nor does it facilitate visual control of the item flow).

4. Items are undifferentiated when they arrive (there is no way to know item priority, due date, complexity, or the effort required; every item comes to the same in-box).
5. Absence of visual cues or other triggers that signal the need for "attention now."

Team's Selected Findings Due to Facilities

■ Each person had a separate cubicle in which to do his or her work (none of the natural workgroup members were near one another.)
■ Similar jobs were clustered together.
■ Few visual indicators.

Though all five barriers to flow listed above were present, the facilities subgroup focused mainly on two aspects of facilities: physical layout and visual management. In practical terms, this translated into the recognition that the current use of facilities hindered flow.

This is the end of guideline 1: Identify waste and barriers to flow. As is now evident, much of the teams work was on this single guideline.

What the Team Learned from the "Remove Barriers to Flow"

■ Locate the point(s) in the workflow where these (waste and barriers to flow) occur

The team had some of this information already documented on the worksheets they used, and in the workflow model they created, as a result of "making the end-to-end flow visible." They identified where in the activity sequence the review and approve activities and queues occurred, and where the value-creating activities occurred throughout the workflow.

■ Determine cause(s) of the waste and why the barrier to flow exists

The team did not spend much time on causal analysis; we all agreed that the time would be better spent designing a different workflow with more desirable features, fewer barriers to flow, and less components. Which they did, and you'll read about it very soon.

■ Develop and implement an integrated set of countermeasures that address the causes and remove the barriers

What is a Countermeasure?

A countermeasure is the response you choose (action you take) to address each "barrier to flow." Each countermeasure is a specific adjustment that addresses the problematic features of the components that currently hinder flow. A countermeasure for equipment that is "out of reach," is to get that equipment in reach. You may move the equipment, move the person, or both.

Often, there is a set of work features from multiple components that *collectively* cause waste and hinder flow. Your countermeasures should reflect this interdependency, and they should be implemented as *an integrated set*, i.e. adjustments that are consciously designed and aligned to complement and reinforce each other. Suppose a workflow is spread across different floors with activities assigned to different people. Each activity has its own trigger. A set of integrated countermeasures may include, co-locate the people to one floor, designate a single work area for this work, establish a single trigger that starts the entire workflow, and provide all the needed equipment and only the needed equipment to that work area, within easy reach of the people doing the work.

As you consider countermeasures, I recommend that you include a time dimension for each. If you visualize a series of time-boxed iterations, such as immediate, or 30, 60, 90 days, you are more likely to make progress sooner and formulate more pragmatic alternatives.

Often you hear the term "future state" or "to-be" process. This often is perceived as a single, one time solution to be rolled out. Of far greater use and benefit is thinking of the future state as a set of incremental changes or iterations that, over time achieve flow targets. In this case, the *initial* future state might be a lead-time of two days for two program offices.

The team came up with a set of adjustments that addressed findings in workflow design, IT, human resources, measures, and facilities that I'll highlight shortly. They decided it was impractical to try to get the Dod to change the regulation regarding Comptrollers. They used the incremental change approach, i.e. frequent small pilots or "trystorms" to implement the countermeasures.

Principle 5: Connect and Align Value-Creating Work Activities

Typically, it takes a set of jobs from multiple functions to accomplish the activities associated with producing a given item in knowledge-intensive work.

Each job is made up of activities, some of which turn out to be value-creating and some that are nonvalue-creating *when viewed in the context of the appropriate workflow* to which they belong. Though several jobs are involved, the total *amount of work* each *activity* contributes to the workflow may be relatively small. Grouping and connecting the value-creating work activities into logical sub-sets and sequences often provides a potential alternative to organize work and resources. The alternatives may or may not match current job definitions or department responsibilities.

In my experience, the set of jobs that make up knowledge workflow have not been consciously defined or designed around their *desired contribution to flow* as an organizing principle. Each job is designed independent of the others, and of the relevant workflows.

To me this situation argues strongly for designing the workflow architecture and the work within, before you design or allocate that work to "jobs."

Five guidelines to connect and align value-creating activities.

1. Locate each value-creating activity
2. Separate the work from the people and systems that currently do it
3. Analyze the work content
4. Examine alternatives to do the work
5. Assess the feasibility and implications of structuring the work and organizing the required resources in this way

What the Team Learned from the "Connect Value Creating Activities" Principle (5)

Locate Each Value-Creating Activity

The team decided that the value-creating activities were associated with four roles (recall the current workflow involved 12 roles).

Separate the Value-Creating Work from the People and Systems That Currently Do It

By separate, I mean "group" all the value creating work together regardless of whether a person does the activity, or whether IT is used to do the activity. The team learned that very little of the value-creating work was actually done by IT. Mostly, IT was used to route information in a serial fashion to each of the 12 roles. This is pure waste.

Analyze the Work Content

Analyze the work to determine if any of the value creating work activities must be done sequentially (interdependent activities) or whether an activity is independent of others, or a combination. Determine how much effort the work represents, how specialized it is, and which part of the work is best suited for people, which is better performed by IT.

The team was able to achieve a dramatic reduction in lead-time when they realized that most of this work was actually collaborative, and could be done by getting the four roles together at the same time to make the decision needed, in real-time. This discovery alone eliminated most of the handoffs, reviews, and queues.

Examine Alternatives to Do the Work

The team settled on an alternative whose main features were collaborative, real-time, and face-to-face, using four people (one for each functional discipline they deemed necessary). Another alternative might use fewer, but cross-trained people since the amount of work was a couple of person-hours. A third alternative would be a scheduled conference call among the four people needed.

Assess the Feasibility and Implications of Structuring the Work and Organizing the Required Resources in This Way

The team concluded that the first alternative in No. 4 above was very feasible. From a technical standpoint, there were no issues. Costs were very low and primarily in the form of providing time to pilot the approach. There were no capital costs.

Thus far, the proposed countermeasures focus mainly on changes to features of the workflow design. The team also thought through implications on other interrelated components so they would align and reinforce the new workflow design. I cover these along with how the team gained leadership support while discussing the "organize around flow" principle next.

Principle 6: Organize around the End-To-End Flow

Two guidelines to organize around the end-to-end flow.

1. Assign operational accountability and responsibility for the workflow *as a whole.*
2. Deploy, operate, and connect the required resources (along the path) so they optimize flow with respect to customer demand.

What the Team Learned from the "Organize Around Flow" Principle (6)

Assign Operational Accountability and Responsibility for the Workflow as a Whole

One of the key ingredients of the team's success was the close involvement of leaders from three functional departments, two of which participated along with the natural workgroups. I believe that, due to this direct involvement, these leaders had a deeper understanding of the significance and implications of the findings and were able to experience directly the energy and enthusiasm of the other team members. This, in turn, helped them become strong advocates and effective champions when it became time to implement countermeasures.

No new roles were created in this project. Other improvement projects may choose to establish the new role of value steam manager or process owner. This new role *owns the design of the set of work components required throughout the workflow.*

In the case of the funding document, the operational accountability and responsibility was shared. The two leaders reached an agreement first. They, in turn, presented a united front to the third. One of the most important objectives for these leaders was to make sure that the work session results became *operational* results. Another objective was to make sure that the natural work group members with implementation responsibility had the time, resources, and political support to run pilot experiments prior to a formal deployment.

Deploy, Operate, and Connect the Required Resources So They Optimize Flow with Respect to Customer Demand

This particular workflow had high demand beginning roughly two months before October. It dropped significantly about two months after October. This is due to the Congressional Appropriation cycle when DoD's annual budget for the government's fiscal year begins. The seasonal nature of the demand was a key influence; the level of resources required is very different during the peak period.

The team was able to secure a conference room that they dedicated to this workflow. The space in the room was laid out so that the people needed could come together as a group and collaborate in real time, to make the needed decision(s). IT system access and monitors, along with other equipment (faxes, phone, and video-conference capability for locations too far to meet face to face) was installed in the conference room. The available time was scheduled so that a time period for individual customers could be reserved. Time periods were communicated to customers so they could arrange their schedules in advance to prepare for the event. The work to be done before, during, and after the event was written down and standardized. Training (with examples) was created based upon the standardized work. Members of the natural work group facilitated the training with their customers and other stakeholders in advance of the event; ideally, it was the kickoff for the decision making cycle which culminated in the event.

Principle 7: Manage the Flow Visually

This principle typically makes real time information on status, progress, problems, and performance results visible to everyone within the flow as part of their daily work. It helps focus attention not only on maintaining the rhythm of regular flow operation, but also on establishing explicitly defined contingencies (i.e., a fast, known, and certain response) for removing barriers to flow when they occur. Often the actual path and the flow of the item along that path are both visible to those who do the work.

This allows everyone within the workflow to self-monitor whether the rate, quality, and quantity of their work is optimized to meet the workflow's performance targets.

Everyone should also be able to distinguish between normal and abnormal operations quickly (real-time feedback) so that defective work is not sent downstream and help can be dispatched right away, when and where it is needed to get things "back to normal" quickly.

Three guidelines to manage the flow visually.

1. Explore ways that each member of the natural work group may view "flow" real-time.
2. Make it easy for each member to spot normal vs. abnormal operating conditions, in real-time.
3. Provide information on item status, progress, problems, and performance measures to everyone throughout the workflow in real-time.

What the Team Learned from the "Manage Visually" Principle (7)

Explore Ways that Each Member of the Natural Work Group May View the Real-Time Flow

The flow occurred in real time during the face-to-face event, so all participants were easily able to see what they had to do during the event. The event-scheduling calendar was posted on one of the conference room walls. This made it clear to everyone whether another event was about to occur in that room, so time awareness was high.

Make It Easy for Each Member to Spot Normal Versus Abnormal Operating Conditions, in Real Time

Everyone was provided with the same written checklist and criteria with which to make the decision. The decision was now made jointly upfront in a much shorter sequence. When the decision was reached, the parties signed a worksheet that accompanied the inputs used.

Provide Information on Item Status, Progress, Problems, and Performance Measures to Everyone throughout the Workflow in Real Time

All of this was done outside the IT system. The results were entered along with the signatures. The routing by role sequence was still hard-wired in the system, but it didn't matter. There was nothing to review and approve and the participants who previously were notified by e-mail at the end of the long sequence were the ones who now came together upfront to make the decision. Data on both cycle time and lead time were being collected and reviewed.

Everyone likes a story with a happy ending. For me, endings are happy when a client continues to achieve the desired results, *after* I leave. While I was working directly with the improvement team, they implemented the revised workflow in 2 of 40 Program Offices. That was several years ago now. As I was working on this chapter I decided to "check-in" to see how this story ended. It turns out that all 40 offices are using the revised workflow.

I felt pretty good when I learned this; I'm especially proud of the team-since they did the hard work. As a taxpayer, you should feel better too.

Please feel free to contact me by e-mail (robertdamelio@sbcglobal. net) if you have a question on the seven principles, or through my Web site (http://www.thebottomlinegroup.com).

Appendix

Overview of Chapter Content

- Five sources of information used to create maps
- Mapping work session guidelines
- Relationship map complete example for Phil's Quick Lube
- Swimlane diagram, complete example for Phil's Quick Lube

Five Methods

There are five basic methods to obtain the knowledge necessary to create a process map.

1. Self-generate
2. One-on-one interview
3. Group facilitation
4. Content (document) review
5. Observation

Method 1: Self-Generate

If you have first-hand knowledge of the work, along with mapping experience, you can create a draft map and have others involved in the work react to it. This method produces a draft faster than the others, but doesn't create buy-in, encourage teamwork, or strengthen the natural workgroup's shared understanding of their work.

Method 2: One-on-One Interviews

A series of one-on-one interviews with members of the natural work group plus selected suppliers to and customers of the work group will enable you to create a draft of the process map. You can then hold a work session with those you interviewed to review (validate) the map. A much less effective validation approach would be to route the map to those you interviewed and others knowledgeable of the process and ask them to review it for completeness and accuracy.

This method works best when the interviewer is well-prepared, is seeking *limited* information, has good questioning and listening skills, is able to rapidly synthesize information, and is flexible enough to adjust on the fly without getting rattled. That is the easy part. I also should add that the interviewer should be politically sensitive, tactful, respectful, able to easily establish rapport, comfortable with clarifying ambiguity, and not be easily intimidated. If you possess or have done the proceeding, this next part is easy: project confidence and provide assurance. You should be familiar with the work (via observation and possibly content review) before you start the interviews.

Note: The group facilitation method (see method 3, below) uses the same skill set as individual interviews, and adds techniques to monitor and balance participation and interaction among the group. It also typically includes designing and conducting context specific (tailored or created for a unique natural work group) individual and group activities or assignments, which help provide individualized feedback and coaching. In my experience, the skill sets I've just described are not adequately strengthened as part of the training typically associated with Six Sigma or other continuous improvement approaches. These skills take deliberate, effective practice and feedback to strengthen and master.

Method 3: Group Facilitation

The third method available to help you create a process map is to arrange for the people that constitute the natural work group to come together in one place to collectively generate the map themselves, with the help of a skilled facilitator/experienced coach. This method provides the greatest direct interaction among the suppliers, performers, and customers that are doing the actual work currently. By using the natural work group, time spent creating the map increases the sense of ownership that the group feels regarding the map and more importantly, the work.

The facilitator/coach provides structure, ground rules, conventions, examples, just-in-time learning, and "expert" observation and analysis skills to aid the natural work group. I believe the goal is to increase the depth of the natural work group's understanding of the work, and to grow or develop their problem-solving capabilities. The map is one useful byproduct. (See also Tips for Creating Process Maps.)

Note: The natural work group is the specific individuals that directly perform the work, and that talk with one another to do that work, regardless of physical location throughout the end-to end-workflow.

Method 4: Content (Document) Review

Often, there are several types of existing content documentation that you may review. There may be formal and informal training materials, briefings, procedures, policy documents, work instructions, job aids, templates, and example work products that are associated with "parts" of the end-to-end process. I think of this as the "scavenger hunt" part of preparation. It is very helpful to compile and organize this information in one place for the natural work group to see and be able to access.

As the facilitator/coach, you are trying to help the work group make sense of the information, which means viewing the set of information holistically and understanding the role, purpose, or contribution each information "part" makes to the other information parts and to the workflow. One tip is to view this information as discrete puzzle pieces; your task is to create the workflow puzzle from the pieces.

Method 5: Observation

There is no substitute for "go and look for yourself," *especially if you know what to look for.*

Most of us have to learn how our customer defines value, and then how to use that knowledge to recognize waste, i.e., to distinguish between value-creating and nonvalue-creating activity. We also must learn to recognize and understand part/whole relationships, i.e., end-to-end flow and portions (fragments) thereof, how work "fragments" are or should be connected (coupling), triggers, and barriers to flow.

Because of the importance of learning to view and think about work in ways that may differ from what takes place currently, I believe it is essential to provide "just in time" learning on "what to watch for" and "why" to the natural work group prior to any mapping or (process) improvement work sessions.

Then, I recommend that everyone in the natural work group observe the end-to-end workflow to apply what they have just learned as part of all map creation work sessions.

If you are the facilitator/coach for a mapping session, then you should observe the workflow before you conduct the "just in time" learning, so that you can provide relevant examples and highlight a few areas that group members should focus on during their own observations.

See Guidelines for a Mapping Work Session below for more on when to apply these methods. These guidelines are primarily for use when working with a group to help them generate a map.

Guidelines for a Mapping Work Session

Before Beginning the Mapping Work Session

Provide a Clear and Compelling Goal for Creating the Map

This is probably the single most important consideration and often overlooked. The goal should be "clear and compelling" to *those who create the map/do the work*. Ideally, the goal is related to the ongoing performance of the work and is stated in quantitative terms, such as "achieve a lead time of two days," or "reduce waste by 50 percent within two months," etc.

Select the Right People to Get in the Room (the Natural Work Group)

- Knowledgeable of (performers within) the process
- Interested in improving the process
- Available and will stay in the room for the duration
- Customers of the process
- Suppliers to the process
- Outsiders (a designated role that is not familiar with the process and sometimes unfamiliar with the culture, someone from outside the group, division, program, or company)

Provide Handouts Showing Naming Conventions and Example Action Verbs

Include relevant symbols, provide completed example maps, provide examples of well-named versus ambiguous work activities, and well-named work items.

Provide "Just in Time" Learning

Explain the type of maps and analysis that the people who create and use the maps will be doing in light of the goal (see above). Consider using a simulation if you are sure it is relevant.

Always Walk the Process

Walk the process, preferably from the outside-in (from customer who receives the work item, backwards to the initiating event or "trigger").

Establish Ground Rules Up-Front and Post Them on a Flipchart

Some suggestions include:

- Map creation method and conventions (on a separate handout and flipchart).
- No "in and out."
- Think rough draft, "first get it down, then get it good."
- Encourage communication.
- Discourage finger-pointing ("no fault" rule applies).
- Go for quantity of information (breadth versus depth).
- Keep a bin list (a list of outstanding or unresolved issues).
- "What goes on in Vegas, stays in Vegas."
- Think "flow," not "Joe."

Use a Room Large Enough so That People Can Easily Move Around

This is dependent on work group size; a minimum of 6 ft. (vertically) *usable* wall space.

Keep a Kit of Supplies Handy, Include Plenty of "Wall" Paper to Write on

These supplies should include Sharpies°, erasers, and Post-it° note pads of various sizes and colors. Also include rolls of mapping paper and masking tape, making sure the tape will work on the surface, i.e., adhere, but not remove the paint.

Use the Natural Workgroup, along with the Observation and Group Facilitation Methods

- See five methods for more on this.
- Always use observation as one of your methods.
- Use a skilled and experienced mapping facilitator/coach whenever possible.

During the Mapping Work Session

Use "Sticky Notes" to Generate Initial Activities, Etc.

It is much easier and quicker to move a sticky note than it is to draw, redraw, or move the information in your draft. Having the information on sticky notes also helps when you may need to group "like" categories.

Arrange the Sticky Notes into an Initial Layout of the Process

"First, get it down then, get it good." (Sticky notes are generally well-behaved, as long as you keep them away from water.)

The general sequence should be "from the trigger through the value-creation sequence to the end item provided to the customer."

Make Multiple Passes through the Work Sequence as Needed, in Light of the Goal for Creating the Map

- One pass to capture the logical relationships, flow, and boundaries (left-to-right sequence, start and end).
- One pass to reflect internal integrity (steps have both an input and an output, surface missing steps, mechanisms, or handoffs, etc.).
- One pass to add data (depending on type of map and types of analysis).
- One pass to note the location and the types of triggers (the signal or stimulus to start the work).
- One or more passes to note location of types of waste and barriers to flow.

Keep a Steady Pace, Monitor Participation and Group Dynamics

- Don't let a particular technology or software application hinder (constrain) your group process or progress.
- Respect everyone's input (contribution).

■ Workgroup creates the map; facilitator acts as a catalyst, organizer, and coach, i.e., provides structure for the map's content, helps the natural workgroup get off to a good start, assists when questions arise, progress slows, or unforeseen conditions emerge.

After the Mapping Work Session is Completed

Document the Map

- Use a digital camera to capture images of the "raw" map.
- Use software to create multiple views of the map to support analysis and interpretation:
  - Waste and barrier to flow views
  - Trigger/priority/synchronization view
- Resource deployment view.

How to Create a Relationship Map

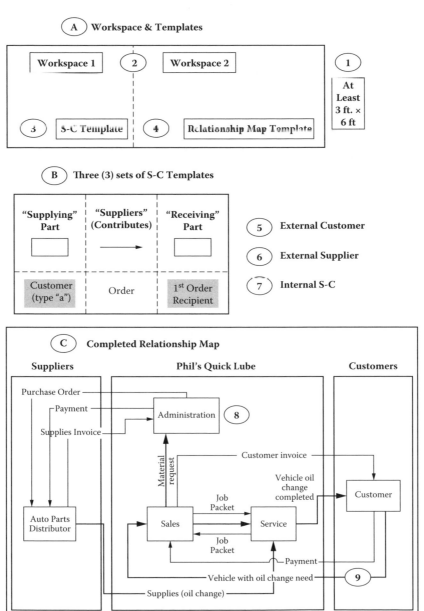

Figure A.1   Overview of the procedure to creating a relationship map.

Table A.1   How to Show the "Organization View" of the "Order to Delivery" Workflow Using a Relationship Map

Step	Figures
A. Create workspaces and templates	A.1
1. Place a large (at least 3 ft. × 6 ft.) piece of paper on a wall or flat surface	A.2
2. Outline two "work spaces" on the paper	A.2
3. Create an S-C template and place it in "workspace 1"	A.3
4. Create a "basic relationship map" template and place it in "workspace 2"	A.3
B. Define supplier–customer relationships (workspace 1)	A.1
5. Define the **external** supplier–customer relationships *first,* starting with the **external customer**	A.4
6. Define the **external** supplier–customer relationships, starting with the **external supplier**	A.5
7. Define the *internal* supplier–customer relationships	A.6
C. Create relationship map (workspace 2)	A.1
8. Draw each part from the S-C template in the corresponding portion of the relationship map template	A.7
9. Draw and label the inputs and outputs, to reflect the **connections among the parts as a whole:**	
• Start with the external customer connections first	A.8
• Then the external supplier connections	A.9
• And, finally the internal connections	A.10

1. Place a large (at least 3 ft. × 6 ft.) piece of paper on a wall or flat surface.
2. Outline two "workspaces" on the paper (Figure A.2).

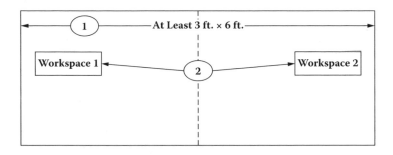

Figure A.2 **"Wall" paper with two workspaces.**

3. Create an S-C template and place it in "Workspace 1."
4. Create a "basic relationship map" template and place it in "Workspace 2" (Figure A.3).

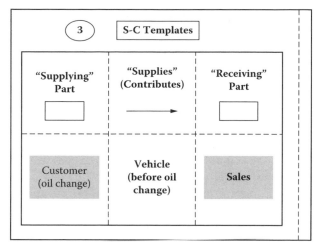

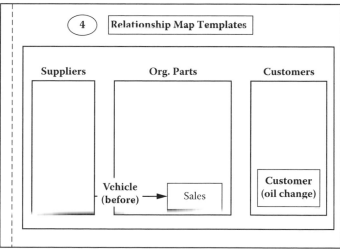

Figure A.3 Supplier–customer and relationship map templates in workspaces 1 and 2, respectively.

Use an S-C Template and Sticky Notes for Steps 5, 6, and 7

5. Define the **external** supplier–customer relationships *first*, starting with the **external customer.** This will give you the customer "touch points" (Figure A.4).
   a. Pick a single (type of) external customer for a specific item.
   b. Determine what the customer provides the organization and what the organization provides to the customer.
      i. Who is the customer?
      ii. What does the organization *first receive* from the customer?
      iii. What part of the organization *first receives* that item?
      iv. What else does the organization *receive* from the customer, *with respect to the first item*?
      v. Which part of the organization first receives *that* item?
      vi. What does the organization *provide* to that customer?
      vii. What part of the organization provides *that* item?

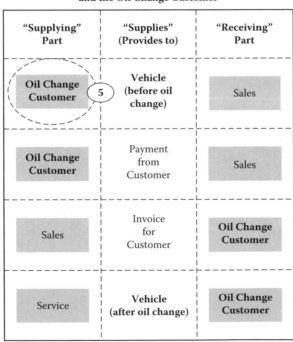

Items that *Connect* Phil's and the Oil Change Customer

"Supplying" Part	"Supplies" (Provides to)	"Receiving" Part
Oil Change Customer ⑤	Vehicle (before oil change)	Sales
Oil Change Customer	Payment from Customer	Sales
Sales	Invoice for Customer	Oil Change Customer
Service	Vehicle (after oil change)	Oil Change Customer

Figure A.4 Phil's Quick Lube customer "touch points" for Order to Delivery oil change.

6. Define the **external** supplier–customer relationships, starting with the **external supplier.** This will help you identify the supply chain (Figure A.5).

   a. For the **same main item**, pick a single (type of) supplier associated with that item.

   b. Determine what the supplier provides the organization, and what the organization provides to the supplier.

     i. Who is the Supplier?

     ii. What does the organization *first receive* from the supplier?

     iii. What part of the organization *first receives* that item?

     iv. What else does the organization *receive* from the supplier, *with respect to the first item*?

     v. Which part of the organization first receives *that* item?

     vi. What does the organization provide to that supplier?

     vii. What part of the organization provides *that* item?

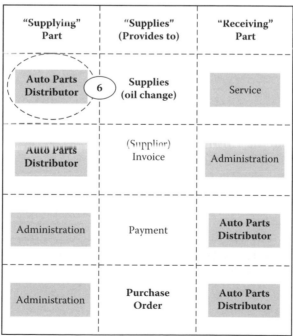

Items that *Connect* Phil's and the Auto Parts Distributor

"Supplying" Part	"Supplies" (Provides to)	"Receiving" Part
Auto Parts Distributor ⑥	Supplies (oil change)	Service
Auto Parts Distributor	(Supplier) Invoice	Administration
Administration	Payment	Auto Parts Distributor
Administration	Purchase Order	Auto Parts Distributor

Figure A.5   Phil's Quick Lube supply chain for Order to Delivery oil change.

Steps 5 and 6 identify the most upstream and most downstream parts of the organization directly involved with Order to Delivery. Step 7 determines what happens in between (the middle of the "stream").

7. Define the internal supplier–customer relationships (Figure A.6).
   a. Starting with the first "order recipient," what happens next?
   b. Which part of the organization is involved?
   c. Then, what happens, and so forth, until you reach the most downstream part (the last part of the organization before the item reaches the external customer)?

Items that *Connect "Part"* of Phil's to another "Part"

"Supplying" Part	"Supplies" (Provides to)	"Receiving" Part
Sales ⑦	Vehicle (before oil change)	Service
Sales	Job Packet	Service
Service	Material Request	Administration
Service	Job Packet	Sales

Figure A.6 Phil's Quick Lube internal supplier–customer relationships for Order to Delivery oil change.

8. Draw each *unique* part from the S-C template in the corresponding portion of the relationship map template (Figure A.7).

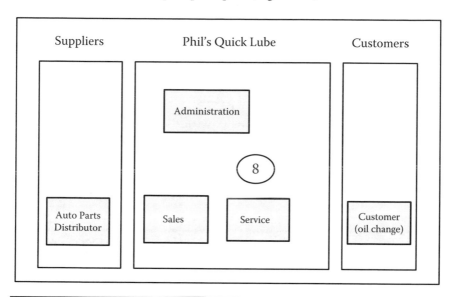

Figure A.7 **"Parts" of Phil's Quick Lube arranged to show Order to Delivery sequence (oil change).**

9. Draw and label the inputs and outputs, to reflect the **connections among the parts as a whole** (Figure A.8 to Figure A.10).
   a. external customer
   b. external supplier
   c. internal connections

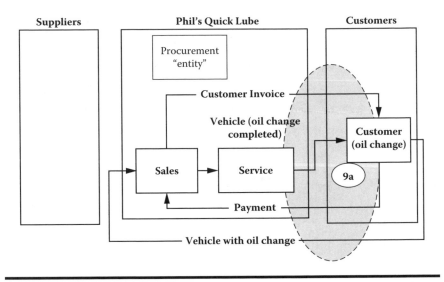

Figure A.8   Phil's Quick Lube with customer "touch points" highlighted.

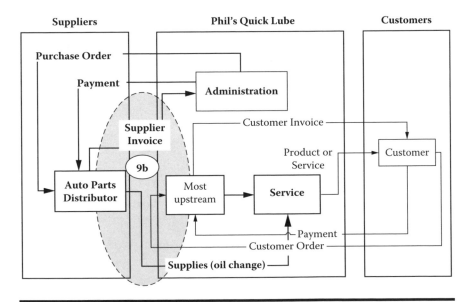

Figure A.9   Phil's Quick Lube with supplier connections highlighted.

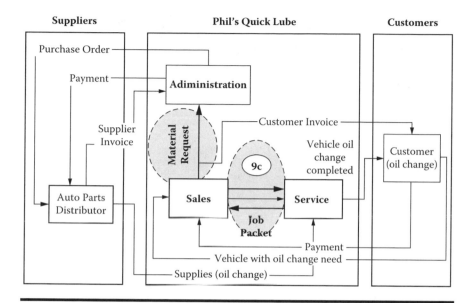

Figure A.10   Phil's Quick Lube with internal supplier–customer relationships highlighted.

Here is the completed relationship map (Figure A.11).

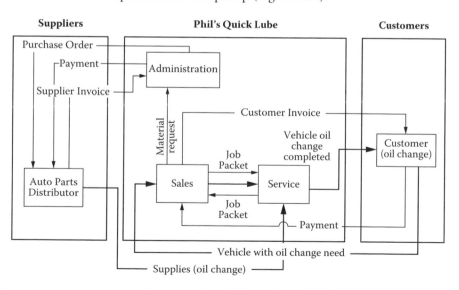

Figure A.11   Organization view of Phil's Quick Lube oil change shown with a relationship map.

How to Create a Cross-Functional Process Map

1. Place a large (at least 3 ft. × 6 ft.) piece of paper on a wall or flat surface.
2. Draw one horizontal band for each "responsible entity" involved in the process (Figure A.12). Bands may be used to represent organization parts or functions, roles, job titles, IT systems, even in-boxes, or other *places where work accumulates*.

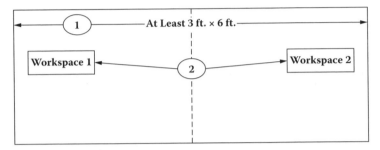

Figure A.12　"Wall" paper with two workspaces.

3. Label the swimlanes starting with the customer (internal or external) from the top beginning with the entities closest to the customer (Figure A.13).

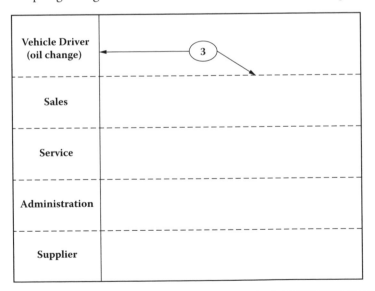

Figure A.13　Workspace with basic template swimlane diagram showing swimlane boundaries with labels and customer swimlane at the top.

4. Ask each group member (individually) to (1) write down the activities that make up their portion of the process on sticky notes, and (2) place the notes on the map in the approximate location where those activities occur in the process (Figure A.14).

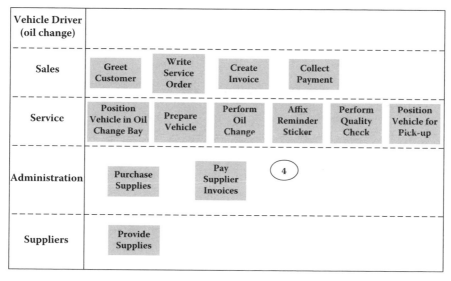

Figure A.14   Swimlane diagram (partial) with activities added using sticky notes.

5. Arrange the Post-it notes so that the group is satisfied that the map reflects the workflow *as a whole* (Figure A.15).

Vehicle Driver (oil change)					
Sales	1 Greet Customer	2 Write Service Order	9 Create Invoice	10 Collect Payment	
Service	3 Position Vehicle in Oil Change Bay	4 Prepare Vehicle	5 Perform Oil Change	6 Affix Reminder Sticker	7 Perform Quality Check	8 Position Vehicle for Pick-up
Administration	11 Purchase Supplies	13 Pay Supplier Invoices	5		
Suppliers	14 Provide Supplies				

Figure A.15 Swimlane diagram (partial) with activities sequenced using Post-it notes.

6. Add and label all inputs and outputs (Figure A.16).

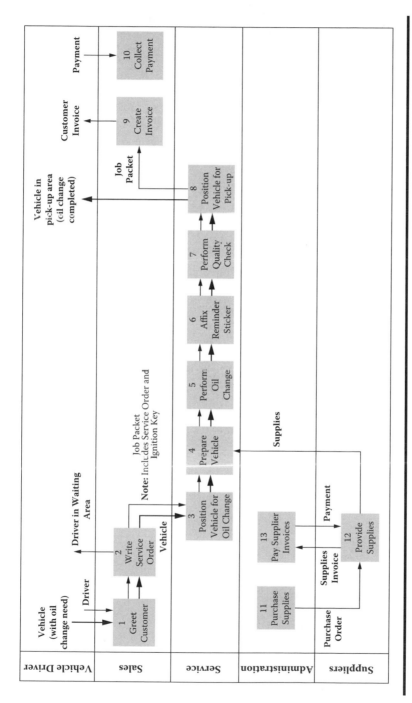

Figure A.16 Swimlane diagram (partial) with outputs and connections added.

7. Use application software to document the map. Take a digital photo of the map on the wall (Figure A.17 and Figure A.18).

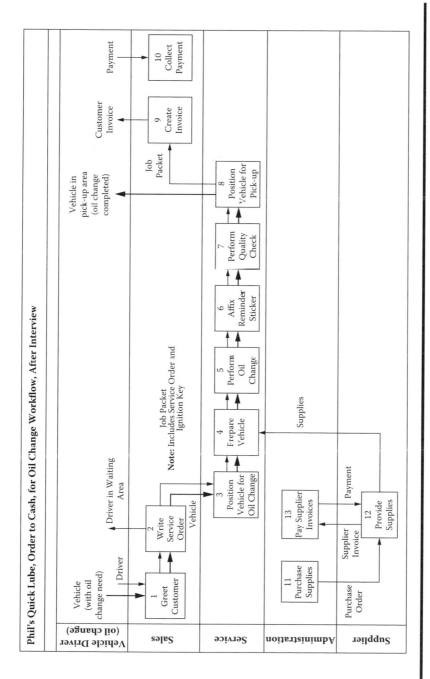

Figure A.17 Cross-functional process map of Phil's Quick Lube interview version.

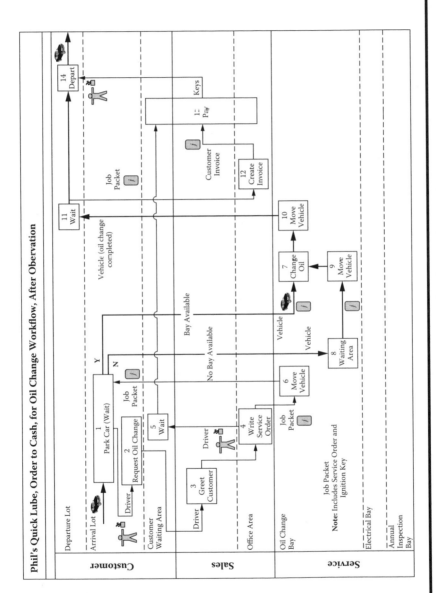

Figure A.18 Cross-functional process map of Phil's Quick Lube observation version.

Index